AUDITION
SUCCESS

WITHDRAWN

Published by ProMind Music
330 West 56th Street, #7-L
New York, NY 10019

BOOK DESIGN BY KEVIN HANEK

ISBN 0-9665993-0-6
Library of Congress Cataloging-in-Publication Data available from the Publisher

Printed in the United States of America
02 01 00 99 98   10 9 8 7 6 5 4 3 2 1

AUDITION
SUCCESS

An Olympic

Sports Psychologist

Teaches Performing Artists

How to Win

DON GREENE, Ph.D.

A publication of *ProMind Music*

In gratitude to all the wonderful artists,

coaches and teachers who welcomed me into their

special world of sharing love and joy through

beautiful and very challenging music.

FOREWORD

MOST OF US WHO ARE performers realize that mental preparation and focus have a significant effect on our performance. However, skills like these are rarely taught. Dr. Don Greene teaches these skills and show instrumentalists and singers how to use and refine them, as they would any other aspect of their technique.

In addition to my career as a concert pianist and conductor, I have taught piano and coached singers for over twenty years. After seeing Dr. Greene's work with members of the Florida Philharmonic, the Miami Opera, and the Lake George Opera Festival, I can honestly say that his ability to enhance performance skills is amazing.

His work with professional and Olympic athletes for the last ten years has made him a leading expert in optimizing physical coordination with acute focus. His more recent work with performing artists has given him a deep understanding of the issues that are crucial to us in rehearsals, auditions, and important performances.

Don's enthusiasm, enjoyment of the artists with whom he works, and his genuine love of music make him a tremendous asset to both professional and aspiring artists. We're looking forward to having him back on the staff at Lake George next season. Our singers and instrumentalists will gain confidence and skill as they learn from him. I'm sure you'll find the same to be true.

— JOE ILLICK, ARTISTIC DIRECTOR,
LAKE GEORGE OPERA FESTIVAL

PROLOGUE

IT WAS A WARM summer evening in Colorado. I had just driven two hours and was going through my garage when I heard the phone ring. I didn't want to answer it. After three days of non-stop work with golfers in Denver, I really wasn't in the mood to talk with anyone, especially some guy asking about my next golf clinic. I told him it wouldn't be until the following month. He asked if I saw amateur golfers on an individual basis and what it cost per hour. When I told him, he asked if I could help him in less than an hour.

He mentioned that he was a bassist playing in the Vail summer concert series. He was an avid golfer, also a musician and didn't have much money. So he wanted to know if I could help him lower his handicap by a few strokes in less than an hour.

I asked him if he could teach me to play the bass in less than an hour. He asked if I could read music; I said that I could read treble clef and asked him if he could putt. I found out that he was really pretty good; he was a seven handicap and actually was struggling with his putting. I offered to meet him the next morning at the local golf course and suggested that I'd work with him in exchange for some bass lessons.

We met on the putting green. I started out by apologizing for my attitude on the phone. I asked him to show me his pre-shot routine for his putting, to go through what he normally did when he was playing, from reading the break and taking practice strokes, to hitting the putt. When I saw what he was doing, it raised more questions than it answered. What did he do under different circumstances, like with longer putts and in more critical situations?

So we went out and played nine holes. I saw him hit a lot of good shots, and also noticed certain things he was doing. When we were done playing, I told him that I was impressed by his swing. I had some thoughts about his putting routine, but I needed more information before I could make any recommendations. I asked him to take two sports psychology inventories that I had been working on; one to measure his learning style and the other to identify his performance tendencies.

He told me that he would take them, but asked if I had any ideas on what he could do in the meantime. I told him that I hadn't gotten my bass lesson yet. He said that he didn't like transporting his stand-up bass all over town. Would I mind coming back- stage after the concert that evening? We could do it backstage. He would leave me tickets at "will call". And he would have the inventories done by then.

The concert that night was great; so was the bass lesson. I wasn't. I had taken some electric guitar lessons, but that was years ago and this was very different. Ed was obviously an excellent teacher, but it really hurt to hold the thick steel strings down for any length of time, as in the bow strokes he had me trying. I soon asked for mercy. No, I couldn't learn to play the bass in less than an hour, but I was certain we could make significant improvements in his golf game, or at least with his putting.

We met in the clubhouse the next morning and went over his computerized profiles. They identified several issues related to his putting difficulties, like not getting a good feel for the length of the putt before addressing it, and his tendency to stand over the ball too long before he stroked it. He was thinking too much before he ever started his putting motion and that caused him to be less than totally focused on actually making the putt.

We went out to the putting green and tried more functional pre-putting routines. It was fairly standard stuff in my practice. An hour later, after he got comfortable with the changes I suggested, we went out and played another nine holes. This time, the results were much different. The first time we played, Ed had 35 putts; now he had only 31. If he could do that on a regular basis, it really would lower his handicap.

After we were done, Ed said that what we had done with his golf game also pertained to symphony musicians; that most of the learning and performance issues were similar to the ones that musicians dealt with every day. I asked for his help rewriting the athlete's inventories in musicians' terms. Instead of asking athletes if they were nervous before a competition, we would ask artists about how they felt before an audition.

That fall, Ed arranged for me to come to the Syracuse Symphony and offer the performing artist's inventories to his fellow musicians. The conductor gave me two minutes to address the entire orchestra before a rehearsal. I admitted that I didn't have any experience working with performing artists, but invited them to take the inventories anyway. I would have their computer printouts the following day and we could start to discuss their profiles then. About forty musicians asked for the inventories and answer sheets.

The next afternoon, we met as a group in a rehearsal room and started going over their profiles. It soon resulted in some very interesting discussions. We wound up running out of time; they had another rehearsal that evening. We agreed to meet again the following day, between the dress rehearsal and their first performance.

By then, several more musicians had asked to take the profiles. The second session was even better than the first. We got into even more fascinating topics, like comparing athlete's peak performance states with their own. They posed questions and raised issues which athletes never brought up. Once again, we ran out of time. Before posting a sign-up sheet for individual sessions, I asked for their written comments and critique.

The Concert Master wrote…"Great work…even a hint of negativity would sabotage the many wonderful things you shared with us." The principal trumpet player wrote about it increasing his awareness and desire to improve, and that it "reaffirmed my belief in life being a journey, not a destination." Another principal described our two sessions as "practical information...an organized approach to concentration, motivation and readiness to play one's best".

I met one-on-one with more than thirty musicians over the next few days. It reconfirmed what Ed had told me about the similarities between playing sports and music. I learned so much talking with these pros about the extreme stress in their lives and how they handled it. Before leaving Syracuse, Ed and I made a few additional revisions to the inventories, to address more of the challenges that symphony musicians confront regularly.

That summer, after moving to Ft. Lauderdale, I addressed the Florida Philharmonic before a rehearsal. This time, I had three minutes to convince skeptical musicians to complete two tests in order to receive some type of feedback, which would take even more of their time. Four brave souls completed the profiles; we had a great session.

One of them was a trombone player preparing for an important audition with the San Francisco Symphony Orchestra. He really wanted to play there and was very ready to move out of Ft. Lauderdale. We agreed to start working together and met one or two times a week for about two months.

We worked through a number of performance issues and both learned a lot. We tried all sorts of things, both old and new. He was doing better and better every week. By the time he left for the audition, he was prepared, confident and ready to win. He played great through the first series of excerpts, and continued playing well into the second. Then suddenly, his mouth went dry. He'd become dehydrated from his cross-country "red-eye" flight the night before. It was very important for him to have enough moisture in his mouth when he was playing. That was it; he was done. He knew it immediately.

I should have thought to ask him about his travel arrangements, but we never discussed them. I know how critical it is for athletes to factor in the negative effects of jet lag on performance, but I didn't ask. We both felt terrible.

That winter, I went back to the Syracuse Symphony to do a follow-up visit. It was great to see everyone again. They took the revised inventories and we talked about our experiences and what we'd learned since we'd last been together. Once again, after the two group sessions, I scheduled half-hour sessions with individual musicians.

One of these was Brian, a 35 year old horn player. I had met with him during my previous visit. He told me that he was starting to prepare for an important audition with the Houston Symphony. He really wanted to play with them and was very ready to move out of Syracuse. He mentioned that he had experienced some difficulties in recent auditions and asked for my assistance. We agreed to work together over the phone after I got back home.

That summer, I was invited to the Lake George Opera Festival to work with the singers. They were just about to start the final week of rehearsals for *Rigoletto*; it was opening in five days. I was able to meet with several of the artists, including a mezzo soprano who had one of the leading roles. She has asked to be called Veronica. She had a challenging week ahead and then some very important auditions.

What follows are the taped conversations with Brian and Veronica, with their express consent. They are as close to verbatim as readability allows. I hope that you learn and profit from their journeys.

CHAPTER ONE

VERONICA AND I MET in a conference room at the high school where they were conducting the final rehearsals of *Rigoletto*. She had already completed the learning and performance inventories, so I brought her profiles. I asked her what she thought we were going to do our session. She laughed...

"...I have no idea."

Do you have any anxieties?

"I don't know..."

Expectations?

"You know, I don't even think I have any expectations. I'm just very curious."

That's good. So please tell me about your background and how you got started in music.

"Umm....I grew up in New England and I studied piano and theater in high school. In college at New York University, I spent my first year at the Tisch School of Arts studying drama. But I wasn't happy, so I went to France for my sophomore year. The University of Paris has a year-long course for foreign students in French history and culture. So I did that, and I actually studied piano in Paris. Then I came back and I switched....is this too much detail?"

No, this is great.

"I switched my major to French. By my senior year at NYU, I started taking voice lessons for fun. I didn't really expect anything from it, but I knew I had always liked to sing. I had done some musicals in high school, so I just did it for fun. But the woman I studied with was very encouraging and gave me tickets to the opera. I really,

really liked it a lot because it had all the elements of things that I had always loved; languages, theater and music, all in one. Plus, I seemed to have a natural ability to do it."

Were those lessons you took regular voice lessons or opera lessons?

"It was all classical music and opera; that was her interest. I didn't even know anything about opera when I started. I just liked to sing. I was with her about a year, and I auditioned for a masters' program at the Manhattan School of Music. It was the Conservatory, and I was accepted. My masters degree took three years because I had no musical education up until that point. So I just got through that, and then after I graduated, I started auditioning for music apprentice type programs and studying all along...and that's been for the last year and a half."

Well, thanks. Would you like to look at your two profiles?

"OK."

We can start with your learning profile. So these are your scores; there are no right or wrong scores, just your scores. First we're going to see if your profile is valid. The initial run-through is just to look at strengths and weaknesses; you're going to have both. If it's valid, then the next time we get together, we'll look for potential solutions to any issues or problems we may discover and hopefully find some practical ways to work on them.

"OK."

Here we go. Your learning profile indicates that you learn best by getting the feel and by trying it, as if to say, 'Let me hear it and then let me go home and play with it. I want to get the feel of it'. Is that right?

"Yeah."

You don't get as much by watching or by people just telling you what to do because you need to try it and get the feel. I would think your best teachers teach you that way. Your feedback preference score of 90 means that you respond best to positive reinforcement.

"Oh, yeah! Isn't that true for most people, though?"

It's true for a majority of people, but not everyone. Some people actually want to know only what they're doing wrong.

"Oh."

Your Caution/Risking score of 75 says that you enjoy trying new things; you're not an extreme risk-taker, but you do enjoy trying new things, and again, back to your trial and experience learning, you want to try and play around with it for a while.

"OK. Hmmm."

Your Willingness to Change score of 85 means that you're open-minded; you're willing to hear new ideas. Your Rate of Change score of 75 indicates that you'd rather move through skill changes faster as opposed to more slowly.

"Right."

Your Commitment to Change of 85 is high. That's good. It means that when you're learning things, you stick with them and give them a chance to work. Even though you like to move along fast, you're willing to stick with it and get it working before you give up on it. That's a wonderful score.

"OK."

Your Outcome/Process score of 85 says that you're interested mainly in results. You're most concerned, even when learning something new, about the ultimate results or outcome. Your

Efforting Level score of 75 is also high, and says that if something's not working, you can try too hard and force it.

"Uh huh."

Your Humor/Seriousness score of 85 is wonderful. That means that you can usually laugh at things and also laugh at yourself. Your Frustration Tolerance score of 60 is tied to this, and says sometimes you laugh at it and sometimes you get frustrated when you're stuck in learning.

Sometimes you can tolerate it and not get frustrated, and other times you can't.

"Yeah."

So you have two ways you can go. If you can laugh at it, have fun with it and not try too hard, then keep on doing it. If you're starting to try too hard, if it's not funny anymore and you're getting frustrated, it's time to leave it alone. Mellow out, go outside until you get your sense of humor back, and then come back in. It'll make learning a lot easier. If the round peg doesn't fit into the square hole, don't just get a bigger hammer!

(both laugh)

"That's a perfect image."

So don't come back in unless you're laughing. It will be better than spending the time grinding and forcing it.

"I know it doesn't do anything. I don't know why I keep doing it."

So stop doing it. Go outside and take a break.

"OK."

Your Practice/Dedication score of 100 means that you have very good habits. In fact, sometimes you probably overdo it.

(laughing) "Yeah. Exactly! I was just going to say that."

So you have a really good learning profile. There are a lot of wonderful things, and a few issues we'll come back to.

"OK."

Let's take a look at your performance profile. This one pertains to your singing on stage, in both rehearsals and performances.

"Hmmm. That's scary."

There's nothing to be scared about. There are a number of really good things on this profile, just like your learning one.

"Oh good!"

First of all, your motivation scores look great. Your Intrinsic Motivation is 100 and your Extrinsic Motivation is 65. That's wonderful!

"What does that mean?"

It means that you're not overly driven by externals; that the prime motivating force for you is from within. You do it mostly for your own pride and the satisfaction of performing your best.

"Yeah."

If those numbers were reversed, with a low intrinsic and a high extrinsic, it could cause problems. The external things are less under your control than the inner ones.

"That's true."

So, your motivation looks really good. Now let's find out what your profile says about your activations levels.

"My what...?"

Your activation or energy levels. They're a combination of your physical and mental energies. They're measured before you go out on stage and while you're rehearsing, performing or auditioning. All of those scores are high; that means you're probably experiencing a lot of adrenalin and anxiety before and during live performances. It says you have a high "rev rate"; that you are highly activated, with lots of energy. You probably come into rehearsals or performances really "up"...

"Yeah. Right."

...and I see that your Optimal Activation is an 80. That's also very high.

"What's that mean?"

It means you sing your best when you're "up". Think of when you're singing really well. Your score of 80 means that you sing your best, or optimally, when you're at a very high energy level. Right?

"Yeah." (laughs)

That's OK, but you can overdo it.

"You're right." (laughs)

You're running your engine at a high rate of speed all the time. That can be draining, and if you go a little past that already high level of 80, then you're into redline.

"Yeah! Yeah!"

You sing your best at an 80 activation level; that's a high energy level. I'm not saying too high, but 85 is probably too high. So if you're already up and if something unexpected happens, you're over the line...

(laughs)

...your cup just overflowed...

"Oh no."

...and that's when you could get into trouble.

"OK. I can see that."

Your ability to activate score of 75 says that you can usually get yourself up for a rehearsal or performance or recital.

"Yeah."

That's good. But your score of 60 for Ability to Deactivate means that at times, you may have trouble bringing your energy level or anxiety down, especially when it gets way too high. So when you need to relax....

"That's really hard for me."

That's my concern with you running at an 80. Because if you're at a 70, you can get from a 70 to an 80 very quickly. I know you can get yourself up easily. But then, if something else happens and you get to an 85, you might not be able to bring it down from the 85 to an 80. And that in itself might cause your anxiety to go even higher.

"Oh God. I'm going to explode. Ahhhh."

But you can learn how to control this stuff.

"Good. I just get so uptight about it all."

Too "up".

"And it's not always positive. Sometimes the 80 is a nervous 80."

Which is no help.

"No."

We'll come back to that. Your Fear of Failure score is 85; that's high. That's fueling your anxiety and saying, 'I'm not sure how it's going to go.' and 'What if I do this wrong?'. Just more fuel for your quick-running engine. You just dumped in some nitro fuel.

"Oh no!" (laughs)

Is it accurate?

"Oh yeah! Yeah!"

Your Internal Distractability score is also high. That means you're thinking too much or too fast. And if you're thinking about what could go wrong, it's going to keep your activation levels high.

That extra thinking and worrying is over-driving your revved-up engine.

"Yeah. Oh, wow."

Your Performance Under Pressure score is 70. That's an average score; it means that sometimes you perform well under pressure and sometimes you don't. In a performance situation, when you're at an "up" and positive 80 and feeling good, then you do well. But when you cross that line and get to 85, or when the 80 is a nervous 80, then you don't perform as well as you can.

"Yeah."

Your Self-Talk score of 60 says that sometimes you stay positive and sometimes you beat yourself up or chew yourself out. Sometimes you're positive and encouraging, sometimes you're self-critical. It just depends.

"Staying positive is a new thing for me. I've only been able to do it for the last six months or so."

How?

"I don't know....I was working with this one coach. He just had the attitude that wherever you are is just where you are. And it's great to be doing what you're doing, that you're up and going forward. He just had a really nice attitude."

Did that feel comfortable?

"Yeah. It felt really comfortable, and so I got used to talking to myself that way. Then one time at an audition, I had this experience where I was so scared that I was shaking. I couldn't even breathe. So I said to myself, 'You know, you must be a very brave person to do this. Even though you're so scared, you're still doing it.' And that's when it really started. Just being able to see how scared I was and yet do it anyway, no matter how it would come out. Just getting up there and doing it anyway deserves...I don't know...something."

Hold that thought. That was a positive spin on the 80 rather than a nervous or negative spin on the 80.

"Right, the nervousness thing."

Physically, they both feel similar. It's just how your mind inter-prets it.

"Exactly. I mean, that didn't make me feel any less nervous nec-essarily, it just made me less down on myself."

It took the nervous edge off, but it left you with the same physi-ological symptoms.

"Right...and then my fear of failure...but there are other voices...it's like millions of voices saying different things..."

We'll get to that. But what you've already done is what you need to learn to do even better; to go into more performance situations with that positive 80.

"OK. But it used to not exist at all."

I just want to support your continuing learning of it, because it's very critical for you to continue the process. But it hinges around how you talk to yourself, and whether you're more positive or nega-tive with your self-talk. We'll get back to that later. Now, your score on Ability to Recover is 80. That's a wonderful score! It means that if you do make a mistake, you can recover and come back; it doesn't devastate you. You can bounce back quickly.

"Uh huh...I just say, 'OK' and go on."

Your Ego Commitment score of 90 tells me that singing is very important in your life.

"Yes!"

Your Self-Confidence score is 70. That's tied to your self-talk. When you verbally beat yourself up, your self-confidence is going to go down; when you stay positive, it goes up.

"Sometimes I have a problem with that, because if I say to myself, 'Yeah, I'm doing great!', I don't want that to be a false way of encouraging myself. Just like 'You're really, really good!'...I don't know if I really believe that or not."

Your self-concept is also affected by your self-talk.

"Uh huh."

How you talk to yourself is going to be a prime factor in your self-concept. And your Self-Talk score of 60 means that your self-talk depends on the circumstances. If it's bad, it's probably negative. And how you feel about yourself depends on how you're talking to yourself.

"Right."

So, let's go back to your self-talk about saying, 'I'm nervous, but at least I have the courage to be here'. Look at your self-concept there as compared to coming out of a performance where you didn't do as well as you knew you could. Aren't those two very different self-concepts?

"Oh yeah. Like both ends of the spectrum."

Your Peak Performance score of 80 indicates that you've probably had a number of incredible experiences on stage and that you know what it's like to perform at those peak levels. And there's no self-critic that goes along on that ride.

"Right. I know. It can go either way. That's really funny; it can go either way."

I'd like to talk to you more about peak performance at some point. But right now, I need to know if you feel your profile is accurate?

"Yeah."

You have some wonderful stuff, like your motivation, your ability to recover and your commitment.

"Oh good."

You have some things that have a lot to do with your thinking, that can work either way. You need to learn how to better use the things that have worked for you, and use them more often. So Veronica, do you have any questions?

"Oh...I don't know. I don't think so. It's funny how these profiles worked. I didn't know how they would work, but they really came up with some good insights."

Good. So when do you sing again?

"I might sing at the dress rehearsal tomorrow night, and in the afternoon it's the rehearsal for the other opera."

Would you like to get together tomorrow?

"Yeah. How about after the rehearsal?"
Great. I'll meet you at the rehearsal hall.

ᔕ

MY MEETING WITH BRIAN, the horn player from Syracuse, to review his profiles was somewhat similar to the one I had with Veronica. Brian and I had our session in one of the backstage dressing rooms at the concert hall. He mentioned that he had recently...

"...set up an audition in Houston that I particularly want, and I'd like to be better prepared. I feel the need to do well. I would very much like it. It's a great situation. I had an audition recently in Detroit and I played well, but I still have this underlying concern that I don't audition well or play well enough at a high level to be with the very best. Deep down, I know I can, but currently I have some concerns. A few years ago, I was making the finals in auditions for several major orchestras. Now I'm not even getting out of prelims, not to mention ever getting close to actually winning a job. And that concerns me, because I'm playing better than I ever have, and yet in auditions, I'm just not doing it."

Brian, would you please tell me about your background?

"OK. Just orchestra...?"

Music school and orchestra.

"OK. I went to Northwestern. I graduated in the class of '81, so I have a Bachelors of Music. No grad school....the rest is just professional experience. I played with the Louisville Orchestra from 1983 through '89. I was the third horn. When I was in school, I played a couple of years in the Chicago Civic Orchestra, which is the training orchestra of the Chicago Symphony. Civic's a big deal; you get to play with the CSO. Although I never did...I never...even though I went through the numbers and paid my dues, somehow I got passed over a couple times. That's something which I've never really totally gotten over. A small part of me is like, 'How come I never got to do that?'. It's always kind of pissed me off a little bit, but playing well is the best revenge. It doesn't exactly hold me back anymore. So I was playing in the Chicago Civic and I was basically just freelancing."

When did you audition for the Louisville orchestra?

"Well, first I auditioned for what's now known as the National Repertory Orchestra. Back then it was called the CPO, the Colorado Philharmonic Orchestra. It was based in Evergreen, Colorado at that time. It's a training program in the summer with nine weeks of intense repertoire, and I was one of three principals there. I won the Louisville audition shortly thereafter. But Colorado should definitely be on the resume, because that's a big deal; the CPO and then Louisville. So I was in Louisville from '83 to '89, and in the summers from '85 to '89, I played with the Colorado Music Festival in Boulder. Going out to Boulder is like Jackson Hole or any of those festivals. You know, like the Teton Festival. I mean, I was playing with players from Chicago and New York and really excellent free-lancers. It was a great experience. Eight weeks of just absolutely great music and riding your bike and hiking and illicit romantic affairs...it had everything."

(laughs)

"I played second and fourth horn, that was my niche and that's fine; I had a great time. As a matter of fact, that last summer in '89, my best friend and I were roommates and we were first and second horn. That's some of the best playing I've ever done in my career. We just tore the place up. It was great. In '89, after he had gotten principal in Columbus, the third horn position became open. He said, 'I know Brian hates it in Louisville, let's get him'. So I made a decision to leave a tenured position; I hated it that much. I knew it was probably only going to be a one-year position. So, from '89 to '90, that one season, I played in Columbus. I had the unique experience, I don't recommend it, of having to audition for your own job. If I win the audition, I keep the job I already had. If I don't win the audition, I lose my job and I'm out on the street. It was kind of the worst of both worlds. I played an OK audition, but it wasn't, you know...even though they knew who it was, they just couldn't hire me. I didn't make it past the prelims. But nobody won the audition. They didn't choose anyone. I was out on the street. So... I switched mouth-pieces, because I wasn't happy with my setup, and three weeks later I won Syracuse."

(laughs) Is that what happened? Really?

"Yeah, yeah, three weeks...I was unhappy. I didn't have a great season in Columbus. I was having some playing problems because I had made some huge adjustments and I switched a mouthpiece. I just changed too many variables, including who I was playing with and where I was living. It was just too much for me to handle and I just wasn't playing well. And I didn't play a good audition. But I got my shit together very quickly and, like I said, three weeks later, I won Syracuse."

Wow!

"I came in on assistant utility horn. It was a two year contract. The previous person didn't come back and I was hired. It was a unanimous decision from my colleagues, so I didn't even have to play, which I felt really good about. They had enough confidence in me, including the music director, that they didn't even make me play a couple excerpts for them as a formality. I was really pleased by that. And then I performed as an associate. Even though the position was assistant utility, my function was as associate. Anytime there was a piano concerto, to spell my colleague, I would play first. I jumped all over the place and that's something I've always been good at. So I was happy...and the first horn was happy... everybody was happy. And then, in the last two seasons, when one of the horn players was getting ready to go to the Atlantic Brass Quintet, I basically filled in on fourth. As a matter of fact, the last two seasons, I was acting fourth horn. It wasn't a change of contract, but I was actually fourth Associate Principal, which nobody does, at least not on a consistent basis. But that's what I was asked to do and that's what I did. I did it very successfully, I think."

When did you start thinking about leaving Syracuse?

"Well, I had always been going to auditions...and it's kind of funny...I knew I'd been playing better than at any point in my career, especially the last couple of years. And yet, I wasn't getting out of the prelims of any of the auditions. I was going for all the big ones like Philadelphia, Chicago, San Francisco...but I wasn't getting out of prelims. I wasn't getting diddly. When I was in Louisville though, I was runner-up for the assistant job in Pittsburgh and the assistant job in San Francisco. I was in the finals for that, and I damn near got the gig."

But that was in Louisville. What about after you got to Syracuse?

"I wasn't getting out of the prelims and it was really getting frustrating because I knew I was playing better than I had before. Finally, I realized that the reason I wasn't getting out of the prelims was because I wasn't preparing for auditions the proper way. That's why I want to work with you. Whatever had worked back then wasn't working now. I decided that it was time to change the game plan."

Tell me more about your last audition.

"Well, first of all, in that audition, I had a new horn. I felt comfortable on it, but I still didn't quite make it. I was disappointed that I didn't do better. I have gone by what my old teacher told me a couple of months ago, that I should just do what I've been taught and what I know. I've heard great players, studied with great players and know everything I need. I just need to trust inside. And I know that I really don't need to go to any other teachers; my tape recorder and I can solve any problems. That's where I'm at."

When is the audition in Houston?

"In about eight weeks. Does that give us enough time?"

Hopefully so. But let's go back to the Detroit audition first.

"I started preparing intensely three weeks before and I think I burned out. I felt myself ramping down in Detroit. I still played a good audition, but I didn't think I was all primed. The thing about Detroit was that I was in a little warm-up room and the person next to me was blasting. All I did was sit back and say, 'This is the first note of Schubert. This is how I'm going to play it.' So I was able to overcome that crummy little room with someone blasting through the excerpts, when I just wanted to sit there and be quiet. Apparently I didn't practice enough, because I still had a mistake on the fifth excerpt. At that level, that's enough. I had made one small mistake in a previous excerpt, it wasn't a bad one, but two mistakes and I guess they figured, 'He made two mistakes. It wasn't what we were waiting for. He's out of here.' and that was it."

Do you know what caused that second mistake?

"I'd been playing well. But I got to the fifth excerpt and they had put the wrong part on the stand. So I was just going along and I tried to relax. It was a loud excerpt and then I felt a little shake in my playing; but I played through it and I thought I was doing fine. The mistake came out of the blue."

Five minutes before you went out there, how did you feel?

"I was very calm and relaxed. I knew what I had to do. They even gave us the list of the excerpts that we would be playing in the prelims. I just psyched myself up more mentally and physically to start with the Schubert. And that went extremely well. It's a part that I've had difficulty with in the past, but I absolutely nailed it. But for the fifth excerpt, it was the wrong part and I was losing a little bit of focus. I played two wrong notes because I expected to see the second horn part, but they put the fourth part to the Tchaikowski, which I didn't remember until later. I'd stopped right in the middle of it and they said, 'Thank you'. I think they were going pull the hook on me anyway. I told the monitor that I would like to do that again. They thought about it for a minute and then said, 'Fine, go ahead'. So I played it again, knowing that this time it had to be better. I started out better, but I still 'chipped' something. They just said, 'Thank you' again. It was a disappointing end to what I had hoped would be a good audition, and what had been going well up until that point."

So, it was otherwise a good audition?

"Yeah, it had been a good audition. Until that excerpt, I thought I was really on a roll. And I was fully prepared to go on and accept that as just a momentary lapse. But I didn't even get the chance. I wasn't the only one, though. I talked to a number of other musicians who also thought that the prelims were very short. But I guess I just didn't play the way I needed to."

Why don't we start by taking a look at your learning and performance profiles?

"Sure. I took both inventories right before I left for Detroit. I could imagine myself very well being in an audition, so these ought to be pretty accurate because this was right before I left."

Most of the categories on your learning profile look just fine. One of your strengths is the balance between your four learning modes, that you learn from watching and feeling, as well as through understanding and from your own trial and experience. Does that sound right to you?

"It does."

You seem to try enough when you're learning something new, without over-efforting or trying to force it if you're not getting it right away. You have a fairly good tolerance for frustration, but your Humor/Seriousness score is too much on the serious side.

"Yeah. I normally have a great sense of humor in life, but with my playing, I think that sometimes my ego gets in the way. It's just that my music is so important to me."

The Humor/Seriousness category is an indicator of whether you're able to keep your sense of perspective, so you can laugh at yourself and not take it too seriously. It's too important for you to take so seriously.

"The guys in my section have been very good at helping me to do that and yet, I really need to make it to a major orchestra. And that's where the seriousness comes in."

Maybe a more helpful way would be to take your humor with you.

"To the audition?"

Not just the audition. The whole process. You know, the big picture.

"It wouldn't be the worst thing if I stayed here the rest of my life.

I've been thinking lately along those lines. There are worse things. But I find myself not wanting to accept that."

You don't need to make it so black or white. You could live with either one. Houston is certainly important, but it's not life or death.

"No, it isn't."

If you win it, you won't be an instant millionaire. And if you were to lose it, you could deal with it. Right?

"Oh sure. I always do."

But move it away from the extremes. It's not going to instantaneously be a wonderful life in Houston.

"No. I've got no illusions about that."

And if you don't make it, there are a lot of good things for you here in Syracuse. But let's finish up with your learning profile. Your Practice/Dedication score indicates that you generally have good practice habits, but both your Mental Rehearsal and Audition Preparation scores are modest. So my question is, were you properly prepared for that audition?

"Pretty much. I started three weeks before. I thought my prep was good, but in hindsight, it wasn't quite good enough. Apparently I didn't practice enough, because I still had a mistake on the fifth excerpt. I guess I could have done a little more mental rehearsal. I think I need to do more of that for Houston."

It's also important for you to start designing the pre-audition routine that you're going to use in Houston; one that will take you on stage better prepared to play your best. Your performance profile should give us some good clues about what should be built into that routine. Are you ready to take a look at it?

"Sure."

There are a number of very positive aspects on your performance profile. Both your intrinsic and extrinsic motivation are strong; you're not distractable by external things; you've got an optimistic outlook and you keep your self-talk on the positive side. Does that sound accurate?

"It does so far."

Your energy levels and your ability to control performance anxiety also look good.

"I think I have the physical stuff down. I did a good job with that in Detroit. I was mostly relaxed, only a little tense. I could feel a little tension in my shoulders, but I still went out and had no shake. I just got a good breath and played."

However, your internal distractability is about five points higher than it should be, and the Fear of Failure score is five to ten points higher than I'd like to see it.

"So, Internal Distractability and Fear of Failure. I was being very honest."

That's good. I'm just concerned with both of those being higher than they should be. Distracting yourself with your own overthinking; thinking too much about what could go wrong. Too much in terms of 'what if?'...

"Like, 'What if I lose the count?'. I do tend to do that, but I would like to eliminate it if I can. I just don't know how to do that."

One possible solution is to give a name to the voice that brings up the 'what if?' questions.

"So I should imagine a person...?"

No, just give it a name.

"Should it be a person from my past or just a made-up name?"

Any name that comes to mind. You can think of him throwing a "what if" at you, like, 'What if I go into this audition and miss the first note?'. Think of that coming into your head.

"OK, so I'm going into the audition and I think, 'What if I bash the first note?'. Then what?"

Just tell me the name that you'd associate with that voice, the one saying that to you.

"Hmm.... just come up with a name? How about 'Bob'?"

Great. Now let's take Bob out of your head and externalize him as the one behind the 'what if?' voice. Think of the things that Bob's been saying to you...

"Alright."

...and for every "what if ", rather than taking it internally and letting it snowball and buying into it, reinforce what you need to do instead. Every time you hear the "what if", respond either with a positive statement or challenge it. You can challenge that externalized voice rather than buying into those doubts. Answer with a very conscious, logical and knowing response.

"And I should make this a daily part of my routine as well? This shouldn't be just a specialized thing?"

That's right.

"You know, with those internal distractions going on, I sometimes forget to focus on creating the sound, which seems to be the way that works best for most excellent players I know. I don't do enough work creating sound; I react to what comes out of my bell as opposed to creating it and imagining it as a finished product before I even physically start. I need to do a lot of that, and I know that, and yet I don't do that. What does that say?"

It says that you need to set up a schedule to practice that. Just like setting up a schedule to physically practice the pieces for Houston, I'd also encourage you to set up some mental practice time.

"I seem to need some help with that."

When would you like to start?

"Well, when do you leave Syracuse?"

I leave here on Sunday. But we can do the rest on the phone, if we can talk once a week. We could start whenever you'd like.

"OK. I'll give you a call in a week or so."

That'll be great! I'll look forward to talking to you then.

"OK. Good bye."

Bye bye, Brian.

CHAPTER TWO

M Y SECOND MEETING WITH Veronica was the next afternoon, when she came out of her rehearsal. We went into
the vestibule and found some comfortable chairs. After
the other singers had gone, we went back to the previous day's conversation. She started out by mentioning...

"...the voices in my head."

I'd like to start knowing more about what the voices tell you to
do in order to sing well.

"Oh."

Think of two or three positive words that would help before you
go on. What words capture your best singing, or what you need to
do? Imagine that you're about to go on stage and you're hearing one
of your teachers reminding you how to sing well. What would they
say?

(long pause)

"I don't know."

How about words like "posture" or "breathe" or "flow"...?

"I think it would be something more...not something physical.
Something like, 'There's nothing to worry about, as long as you're
thinking about the character and what the character has to do. Then
there's nothing to be nervous about'. Something like that."

We're not talking about nervousness yet, just your good singing.
What do you need to do to sing well? Or what do you do when you
are singing well?

"There are certain things I do. I would breathe in a steady
way..."

So..."breathe"?

"But if I tell myself, 'Breathe in a steady way', it doesn't work. It just doesn't work. It has to be something...I just have to relax a little bit."

Relax what?

"Everything..."

So if you said, "relax" to yourself, what would it convey?

"I'm not really sure."

Tell me about one of your best performances.

"Uhhhh...I did a recital last year, my graduation recital from the conservatory."

Why were you so good that day?

"I felt like everybody in the audience was really excited to listen to me."

What else?

(long pause)

"I was pretty well prepared..."

What did you do with your voice? How did you sound?

"Pretty good...I was a little nervous, but not...you know. I listen to the tape now and I know I could sound better, but at the time..."

What would you do to sound better?

"Breathe better."

Define "better."

"It helps my voice...it helps support the tone."

How do you learn to breathe better?

"I don't know...by working at it."

We'll come back to this. Let's talk about your fear of failure.

"OK."

Let's assume that you're about to step out on stage and you're thinking about what could go wrong. What comes to mind?

"Things like, 'What if I crack on a high note?'...'What if I forget the words?'...'What if I don't express the aria very well?'...things like that."

Alright. There are two ways to deal with these. Do you work with any younger singers?

"A little bit with high school girls."

Let's say that you've been working with one of them for several months and then it's time for her to do a high school performance. Ten minutes before she goes out, she says, 'What if I crack on the high note?' What would you tell her?

"Oh God....oh God! You can't tell her that she won't..."

What could you tell her to do to prevent that from happening?

"I don't know. This is really hard."

When this happens to you before you go out, and you accept the "what if's "as real possibilities, it can drive your activation level of 80 up to a 90.

"Yeah...."

And if, at that point, you don't have a strategy to bring it down from the 90, it will stay there for quite a while, especially by thinking about it without any solution. So, wouldn't you rather talk about it now?

"Oh, yeah. (laughs) I'm just shocked that I can't come up with anything."

Let me use a sports example.

"OK, I like sports examples."

Have you ever watched any platform diving?

"Like in the Olympics? Yeah."

On back takeoffs, divers stand with only the balls of their feet on the platform. From that position, they can do back dives or inward somersaults. When they're doing inward two-and-a-half's, they spin in toward the platform. One of their fears is hitting their head. Now if they're standing there and thinking, "I hope I don't hit my head," it's very tough for them to go.

"I bet."

Coaches certainly don't want them to get too close, but they don't want them to be too far away either. If they push back too far, it's difficult for them to make the rotations. Then they don't spin enough, and hit the water "short". That can be painful. So, the coaches want them jumping it in the right place. They use positive cue words. Rather than having them think about hitting their heads, they tell them, "Jump to the right place". If they do that, they'll be safer and start the dive well. So instead of thinking, "Don't hit your head", they say, "Jump right", as a positive cue.

"I see."

If they start thinking, "What if I hit my head?" and, "That would really hurt", it can lead to them thinking about being in the hospital. That would probably drive their activation level to a 90. Then they get physically tight and that makes it even tougher to do the dive. So they've learned to substitute positive process cues for each one of the "what if's". For, "What if I hit my head on the platform?", they substitute, "Jump in the right place".

"So in terms of singing....?"

Positive process cues would be more helpful for you to think about than cracking on the high note. So what do you need to do to sing well?

"Well, I need to breathe, I need to relax...and I need to get into my part."

That takes away the anxiety.

"Yeah. But what if I tell myself that and then I don't do it?"

That's just another "what if".

"Oh, no!"

When anxious situations come up, when the stakes are higher and there's more pressure, the "what if" gets louder and faster and you hear it more often. You can take it too seriously and start to buy into it: "Well, what if it does happen? What if my voice cracks?". Once you buy into it, your activation levels rise dramatically.

"Yeah, I see what you mean."

But you can challenge that and start dealing with it. Imagine yourself thinking, "What if I forget the words?". Now, rather than buying into it, I would like you to challenge it and prove why it's not going to happen.

"I'm not going to forget the words. And so what if I do?"

How about, "I've memorized the words. I've spent the time. I've gone through a thousand rehearsals. I know it in my sleep." How's that?

"That's better than, 'What if I forget?', that's for sure."

Or you could use your good sense of humor.

"I think that happened to me before that recital, actually. I was just out there saying to myself, 'There's a whole group of people here to hear me sing. This is crazy!' And I just started laughing because I didn't believe that you could do something like that. You just had to laugh."

And your nervous activation of 85 went down to a 70 or 75.

"Yeah. That's so exciting to actually believe that that can happen."

You did it! Your humor is a definite ally. When your humor kicks in, it's wonderful. But when you're too serious, when the "what if's" are really dominating your thoughts, you're not laughing and your nervousness goes up.

"Yeah, it's stupid. Then you make yourself do things wrong. I swear! You're home and you sing through the arias before an audition and everything's fine, and then you get to the audition and you go, 'I can't do it. I can't do it right.' You make yourself screw it up."

Or you can allow yourself to sing well.

"Right, right. It's not that bad."

Well, we're scheduled to get together again tomorrow at 1:00. Is that still good?

"That's fine. Thanks."

You're welcome. I'll see you tomorrow.

৯

MY FIRST PHONE CALL WITH Brian was the week after I got back from Syracuse. He was anxious to continue. I started by asking him if he had any afterthoughts from our session in Syracuse. He recalled that we had...

"...hit a number of things. I remember you talked about my fear of failure and its relationship to internal distractability. We had discussed Bob. As a matter of fact, I used him on Saturday night. He's the 'what if' guy, you know. 'What if you miss this note coming up?' 'What if you lose the count?' I just told him to back off."

And how did that feel when you said that?

"That felt pretty good. I felt a little more in control."

Super. Did that add any humor to it?

"Actually, I took it as kind of 'professional'. You know it's like, 'Look Bob, I've got to do my job. I'm supposed to get all the right notes, so let's talk about this at a later time'. This was the first time I've tried that exact strategy out."

Good! Now let's talk about the specific dates.

"OK. Today, I got my packet from Houston. The dates are the 20th, 21st and 22nd of May. I've already made my reservations."

That gives us a little less than six weeks.

"I'm going to request a mid-morning time on Monday the 22nd. That's the last day and the finals are later that day. So I'm hoping that I will come in...they will be tired, but I know they're a good section and they'll still be listening. So if I can go in there and prime myself, just walk in there and say, 'Boom, there it is', they'll take me, no matter how many they have in the finals."

OK.

"So I really go in and knock their socks off. No matter how many finalists, they'll add one more if I show them that I've got something."

Have they told you what pieces to prepare?

"Houston has like about 25 or 26 excerpts. But they can throw anything at you they want and they all have to be perfect, that's all. No problem."

What would you like to do to prepare for it?

"In the next week, I would like to get my practicing planned out as far as doing specific things, not just going over the excerpts a number of times. I have thought of taking maybe the top five excerpts that I don't play as well as I would like to, working on at least one of them a day, and really working them over as far as playing them backwards, playing them through the tuner, playing for the tape, playing them slower or faster, playing them in a different key, all sorts of ways you can do it. But there are a couple of excerpts, like the opening of *Rheingold,* that I just don't have in my grasp like it ought to be."

Could you put the excerpts into three piles? One that you could nail in your sleep, one that you can do half-awake, and the third one we'll call challenging. And after you've done that, randomly pick one or two pieces from the first pile and play them, and then move to the second, and then play a few of the picks out of the third.

"Practice two out of column one, two out of column two. Two from each column? At a single practice session?"

Yes.

"Should I work them over or just play them once or twice through?"

Right now, whatever seems appropriate, but separate this practice from your regular playing. And start building a routine into your practice and playing.

"But I play just excerpts and nothing else."

If you're doing scales or practicing other pieces before that, please take a break and go out of the room. Or even better, go outside before you start this audition prep routine.

"So make this a complete break? Because otherwise, I can start right in. Sometimes I'll do that with excerpts, as if it's the first excerpt of an audition. No warmup even, sometimes. I'll just walk in and see what I can do."

Separate it so that you're doing it for a specific purpose.

"Any particular length to this session?"

What would be your longest time on stage for an audition?

"In an audition, probably the longest would be in a prelim, probably ten to twelve minutes max."

Then go for twenty minutes, so you can play longer than you'd ever need to. You could build up to it over several days, certainly by the time we talk next time. In the meantime, just go in and play under the same conditions as you'd expect in Houston. If you're going to be standing in front of the music stand or sitting down, then do that and whatever else will help to approximate the circumstances. Come in with your horn, go through the excerpts and play your best.

"Now is that the session to do two of each from the three piles? That's this kind of practice?"

Yes. And before you go in, check your energy levels and see where you are. Are you going to be playing behind a curtain?

"Yeah, there's always a screen."

OK, imagine that the people on the other side of the screen are there...

"So imagine a screen..."

...and imagine those people and doing it for real. If you feel any anxiety, amplify it, bring it up. Put some pressure on yourself to play incredibly well.

"OK."

But first try to quiet your mind. Deal with Bob or whatever you need to do to get there. And start using a routine so you can find one that works.

"Now this is the checking energy levels?"

Yes, a scan of your body to check your activation level and also make sure that your muscles are relatively relaxed.

"But I put the pressure on myself. That's kind of opposite, isn't it? Because I'm trying to relax myself."

Put the pressure on and then alleviate it.

"All in the same pre-audition routine?"

Yes.

"So put the pressure on myself, imagine the screen, imagine everything else and then quiet my mind and relax my body."

And give yourself some positive cues, words that would catch how you want to play. These would be your process cues. In other words, what are some of the major things that you need to remind yourself of, or your teacher would remind you that pertain to your best playing.

"Mine would be 'I am relaxed and confident in my performance'."

In your routine, use "relaxed and confident". Just say it over and over to yourself.

"And this is after I've put pressure on myself?"

Yes.

"So what I'm doing is getting myself keyed up and then bringing myself down and then stepping into the practice room...."

...and playing to the best of your ability. This is not a regular practice with warm-ups and technical exercises. This is Show Time.

"So that's when I actually walk in and play one from each level."

Yes.

"And I play them in that order? The ones that I can nail in my sleep and then the ones that are marginal and then the ones that are difficult."

...say, "the ones that are challenging"...

"Yeah, I know that's important."

Eventually, you're going to give every excerpt a word. But we're not quite there yet. By next week, will you be able to play all of them?

"Oh sure. I mean I could do this, perhaps even twice a day."

Just go in there after your routine, go through the excerpts, play your best and finish. Go back to whatever else you were doing, and if you want to go through it again later, start with your routine again.

"Should I tape it? Because taping makes me nervous, even sitting at home."

Yes.

"Ok, tape it and then listen to it afterwards."

And write some notes.

"OK, critical listening."

Not critical as much as what you need to improve, how you can do it better next time.

"So put it in positive terms; 'tone could be smoother' or, 'slur could be more in tune'. Something like that?"

There you go!

"Not, 'That sucked'... 'This was terrible'... 'Where'd you get that shaky sound?' Sometimes I listen and say to myself, 'Oh, you've got to be kidding!'. Sometimes when I play the tape, I notice, even sitting here in my living room, when I put the tape machine on and let the pause button go, it's a little different."

The last thing, Brian, is when you're playing these, if you make a mistake, do whatever you'd do if you were to make a mistake in the audition.

"Got it. Just go on."

Just go on. You're going to make a mistake in practice and then you can figure out how to keep on going and build that into your practice. So once you walk into the room to start, you're on. Do your best.

"Yeah, matter of fact, I might go as far as to let the tape go before I get into the room so I don't have the official thing of starting the tape by hitting the pause button. It will make it as close to the real thing as possible."

That's great.

"What else?"

The other thing is to keep notes when you're listening afterwards. Not just on the sound, but on what you've been working on and your progress, and what you've been experiencing and learning.

"So you want me to keep a training diary?"

Yeah.

"I like that idea. You know, I did that once in a while, even as a student. But it was sporadically, I certainly haven't done it lately. But I know it helps."

You can start anytime you'd like.

"Give me a specific day."

Two weeks from today.

"Great. Now I've got a deadline. I work better when I've got some time limits. I've got the whole week off and sometimes I'll fritter it away. So that's probably enough for me for now. I'll call you in two weeks."

That's great, Brian. Take care.

"Bye bye."

CHAPTER THREE

I WASN'T ABLE TO TAPE my last discussion with Veronica before leaving Lake George. We talked about a number of issues and potential solutions and agreed to continue working together on the phone after we both got home. She called me from Manhattan a few weeks later.

"Hi, Don. How are you?"

Just fine, Veronica. It's good to be home. How did it finish up in Lake George?

"Umm...pretty good. Things went really well, but it was really hectic the last week. A lot of rehearsing, and then we had the double billing after the second opera opened up. It was pretty good, though. It was a good experience up there; it's a nice place to work."

Did *Gianni Schicchi* go well?

"Well, the first performance didn't go that great, but the second performance did. So at least we left on a good note. (laughs) It was pretty stressful."

Were there only two performances?

"Yeah. The two shows. But it ended up great so I look back at it with good feelings (laughs)...mostly. Compared to other places I've worked. Ugh! So I've just been home and I've been working on some of the stuff we talked about. It really did help me through *Gianni Schicchi* and the remaining performances of *Rigoletto* a lot."

Can you be more specific?

"Well, before I would do any performance, I was so concerned about what the audience would think of me. I wanted to make sure I would do stuff that they would like. It was kind of going on subconsciously but I thought, 'That's not going to help me perform the way I need to if I'm worried about what they're thinking'. So at least I really, really tried to see that that was what I was feeling, and to try and just push that away. I think it did help, that I could give myself permission not to have to worry about what they were thinking. And it worked up there in Lake George."

Great!

"Where it didn't work though, was in a couple of auditions that I did this week. Because I thought, 'Hey, great! I'm good now! No problems. I'll be able to deal with it and not get nervous and not lose focus'. But particularly in an audition yesterday, I sensed that when I was singing, they weren't interested, the people that were listening to me. And that made me lose my focus on what I was doing. It made me think that what I was doing was uninteresting. In the second piece I sang, they were interested, so it made me more interested in what I was doing and I felt better about what I did when I knew that they liked what I did. But I wasn't happy that I had to have their approval of what I was doing in order to per- form well."

What was this an audition for?

"It was for a management/agent type of thing."

When you say that you sensed that they either liked it or they didn't, what do you mean?

"Oh, just in their interest. I could see that they were looking around. I don't know exactly. They just didn't seem interested. Looking around, doing other things, possibly thinking about things other than me singing."

I've got you. And the second song was better?

"Yeah. I could see that they were paying attention and smiling and thinking 'Oh, yeah! We like this." I found out afterwards that they didn't think I should be singing the first piece. They did think that I should be singing the second piece. But I don't feel that way; I feel like I should be singing both pieces."

Are these pieces you chose or ones that they chose?

"I chose."

But you felt fine with both pieces before you went in?

"Yeah. I felt fine, perfectly fine. But I know that their interest in what I was doing affected my performance. I was upset that I lost my focus so easily."

Well, that's an issue that we haven't talked about yet. We'll need to discuss the difference between an outside-in orientation and an inside-out focus. Do you have some auditions coming up?

"Yup. A big one coming up on Labor Day weekend. I'm going to Chicago."

And what's that one for?

"For the Lyric Opera of Chicago. They have a young artist program. They auditioned a bunch of people in May and June. Then they have a final round where they fly in twenty people and have them sing for the artistic director of the company."

Well, good. When do you want to start working on that?

"Oh, as soon as possible."

(both laugh)

Let's go back to our discussions. We talked about process cues like "relax "and "breathe", and that these are better than the "what if's".

"I keep on thinking about how you said that my activation runs at an 80, and that's what I felt yesterday. I am just too hyper right now. I have to calm down. What we talked about worked for me in Lake George. I was able to calm down. This audition yesterday, I didn't know how to calm myself down. I don't know...I tried everything. I didn't know what to do."

When you talked about the first and second performances of *Gianni Schicchi*, you said the first one wasn't so good...?

"I had a hard time in the first performance really just focusing on what I had to do. I kept thinking of what was going wrong with other people in the cast and I also kept thinking, 'Oh, the audience isn't enjoying this' or, 'I didn't sing that as well as I should have'. I just couldn't do the job that I had to do."

So you were worrying about other singers and also about the audience?

"Yeah. Just feeling like I wasn't making any kind of impression."

And the second performance?

"With the second one, I felt the audience was enjoying it and people around me seemed to be a little more excited about doing it. I just focused on what I had to do."

Aaaahhhh...process cues and an inside-out focus. We really did-n't spend much time talking about routines. Do you understand what I mean by a pre-performance routine?

"No."

You will.

"Oh, I bet I will!" (laughs)

And we didn't talk about centering either, did we?

"No."

So when is your Chicago audition?

"It's a week from Saturday."

How many pieces do you have to prepare?

"Four. One's an aria from *Carmen,* one's a Rossini aria, and one's a Bernstein. And then there's another Rossini, so there are two Rossini's."

OK. How can you differentiate between the two?

"One is much more light-hearted and one's more serious."

Can you rank them in terms of how confident you are when singing them? Say the aria you're the most confident about is a "one", the next one is a "two", the next is a "three" and the one you're least confident in singing is a "four". Can you do that?

"Yeah. The serious Rossini would be a 'one', the light-hearted Rossini would be a 'two', the *Carmen* a 'three', and the Bernstein a 'four'."

And you have all four of them memorized, and you're singing them all?

"Yeah."

Good. When I talk about a pre-performance routine, I'm talking about what you do in the last ten or fifteen minutes before you go on, whether it's on stage for a dress rehearsal, a recital or an audition. The last ten or fifteen minutes.

"OK."

For each of those pieces, I want you to come up with cue words that are meaningful for you about how you need to sing them well. Or how you sing when you're singing your best. Take the more serious Rossini. Give me two or three words that capture either why you sing it well, what you need to do to sing it well, or how you sing it when you're singing it well.

"Oh, I see. So how.....?"

It goes back to the cue words, which for you were "breathe" or "relax". But these need to be more specific for each individual piece.

"OK. So two or three words about how it is when I sing it well."

Or what you need to do to sing it well. Try not to get too technical.

"For each aria?"

Yes. But now for the toughest one.

"Uh oh!"

(both laugh)

I need to teach you a centering process to bring your energy down. Have you done any type of meditation or relaxation training?

"Uh, not really."

OK. You're about to.

"Oh, God."

(both laugh)

It won't hurt! The good news is that you already know how to breathe from your lower abdomen.

"Oh, good!"

Because this technique is based upon proper breathing technique.

"OK."

For the next couple of days, I want you to lay on the floor and put your one hand on your stomach and one hand on your chest, unless you can just do this automatically. Do this deep abdominal breathing for three, four, or up to ten times a day, with your stomach rising without your upper chest moving.

"OK."

So the first sequence of breaths is proper abdominal breathing for up to ten breaths. That's step one.

"OK."

Also, I would like you to breathe in through your nose and out slowly through your mouth.

"OK."

Number two is going to sound a little bit weird to you, unless you've taken Zen.

"No, I haven't."

(both laugh)

OK. You're going to have fun with this one. It's going to be a little bit of a challenge. Have you ever heard of Chi, the life force, or Ki?

"I've heard of it."

Well, it originates from your center. Your center is defined as two inches below your naval and two inches into your body.

"OK."

So lay on the ground and put your hand two inches below your navel and push in a little bit so that you can define that point. And then while you're taking those ten breaths, bring your focus to your hand and be at your center. Get out of your head and into your center.

"Yeah."

If it helps you to close your eyes, then close them. Leave the external surroundings, get out of your head and get there.

"That's probably a bit difficult."

This is your challenge. Don't get critical about your performance. There are no right or wrongs. You're not supposed to nail it the first time.

"OK."

So have some fun with it, and we'll see. Does that sound alright?

"Yeah!"

This will be a big part of your pre-performance routine. It'll help you relax more and get more focused after you learn how to do it.

"OK."

So we've got to go through a learning sequence and what we're doing right now is just doing parts. These will be parts that we're going to build on. In the meantime, play around with it. Does that make sense?

"Yeah."

Do this several times a day.

"Do it every hour?"

You can if you want.

(both laugh)

And also come up with process cues for each of the four pieces.

"OK. Can I call you on Friday?"

That's good. Please get a pad or a little notebook and keep some notes on this stuff, and if something comes up, you'll remember it when we talk next time.

"Yeah. Great! So I'll talk to you on Friday."

Very good, Veronica. Take care.

"You too. Thanks! Bye bye."

Ꭿ

BRIAN, TWO WEEKS LATER. Please bring me up to date on what you've been doing.

"Well, I started my training diary. It was kind of sporadic. Saturday I hardly did anything. I had a gig on Sunday, which was interesting because I had written down that I was playing first and it was kind of early morning and I had to do a lot of lead, giving down-beats and stuff and I'm not always comfortable doing that. I practice that kind of thing but don't enjoy it too much. I wrote down some good things and some bad things. It pretty much mirrored my physical and mental state. Some stuff I played great and some stuff wasn't, but I managed to maintain control, which I considered a victory. But it's not so much nervous as it is that I use too much tension. I think I've been able to differentiate between the two."

Oh, that's good. What does the tension feel like?

"The tension feels like when I take my air, I start shaking. When I play, I start shaking and then I start worrying about it and it gets worse. So what I did in the Gabrielli, I was shaky during the whole Gabrielli…I don't know what set me off, but I just kept going. I didn't miss any notes because of it and I didn't let it get any worse. But I didn't have the skills to get it any better, so the whole piece pretty much remained like that."

So, you take in air and that makes you feel shaky?

"I probably don't take in enough air and that's part of it, so what it is is muscular tension and it's kind of a vicious circle. If you don't take enough air and you use too much tension to play, your muscles start rebelling, I suppose."

And where do you feel that? Which muscles?

"Well, where I feel it, in my playing, is in my lips. Like, if I take a breath and I'm ready to play, it feels like the embouchure isn't steady."

And what do your chest and shoulders feel like?

"You know, my arms will feel a little shaky also, from the tops of the shoulders down the arms, and when you feel like that, you stop breathing because you start focusing on your shakiness rather than what you ought to."

Right.

"What I tried to do was continue to focus on my breathing. I couldn't get it any better, but I prevented it from getting any worse."

While that's going on, what are your thoughts?

"Well, it kind of surprised me because the gig had been going fine and all of a sudden it came out of nowhere, so my thoughts maybe a year ago would have been, 'Oh, great! Here it goes again!'. But I made a concerted effort to just say, 'OK. Here's what's going on. You know what to do'. I hadn't practiced enough to calm down and take better breaths. I did it to some extent, but not enough apparently to effectively combat it and bring myself back to normal. But I did prevent myself from getting any worse, so it was really not that bad. I noticed it, but I don't even know if anybody else noticed it. And I didn't miss any notes as a result of it, which was definitely an improvement."

Good.

"But, yeah, I would say that the arms feel kind of shaky and that makes me breathe less and be less confident in my breathing and then, instead of thinking of the sound of the next note coming in, I worry about everything else. But I did not do that Sunday morning, so that was good."

We'll come back to this. What else did you follow up on?

"I had a couple of things that I want to discuss with you. I wrote some notes. In general, although yesterday and so far today, I've made improvements, I need ways to incorporate more mental work and visualizing into my practice routine. Even though I discussed that with you before, I know that I don't need to go see a teacher. I know everything I need to know. I've studied with the best and I've got notes and lesson tapes from the best teachers in the business and they taught me well, but for some reason, I don't seem to do these things. I don't follow the notes and I don't do enough mental work. I'm definitely physically-oriented, and I've had a number of the teachers tell me that. That's not all bad, but yesterday I really made a concerted effort to incorporate more mental training into my practice and I was somewhat successful."

Does it feel good when you do that?

"Yeah, it does. For example, for Monday I wrote down thirty minutes of notes in my training diary, then I did an hour of audition practice with some relaxation thrown in. I did fifteen minutes of just experimenting. I was watching TV...practicing with the television on is good once in a while...and I played part of a lick that I've been having difficulty with. I just tried to run it through different variations while not focusing on it. Then I did twenty minutes of listening to the only time that I did the audition prep training, the one that we talked about two weeks ago. I listened to that. I did it on Thursday and finally listened to it yesterday. And then I did forty-five minutes of solid practicing."

And how was that?

"Some good things and some bad things. I was most picking licks apart. I focused on a couple of licks and did them in different ways. I had the metronome going and taped things a couple of times. Yesterday I would have to consider a very good day. But lately, I've had a lack of motivation. Part of it's because I had viral pleurisy in my right lung and that knocked my whole vacation off. I wrote down, 'I know what to do. Why am I not doing it?' in my training diary."

What's the answer to that?

"I'm not motivated. I know what to do but I'm not doing it because I'm not motivated. I also put down a lack of focus and organization in practice. I need ways to add structure. I was going to look to you to help me. Maybe if I organized my training diary a certain way and got a practice routine going, the two would help each other."

You might want to commit to following a routine with your practice.

"Which I do not have. My practicing has been sporadically brilliant, like getting ready for an audition. But in general, I have really fallen off the habit of organized routines."

Are you ready to start now?

"Yes. Actually, I kind of started it yesterday, but I want to keep it going. So give me some parameters."

Well, I can't. You're the only one who knows them. When you decide what it is, commit to it, write it down and follow it.

"So a regular time..."

Yes, a regular length of time and a general structure of what you want to do within it.

"OK. One thing I did that was positive was that I took my clock off the living room wall. And what I do is set the alarm and say, 'OK, I'm going to do such and such minutes' and then I don't look at the clock or my watch until the alarm goes off. I find that that's effective."

That's good. The other thing, Brian, are your goals really clear?

"No. I mean the long-term goal is going to the audition and getting the excerpts, but that seems somewhat vague in a way, because I don't seem to be able to practice effectively toward the long-range goal."

You need to make them more immediate and real. Even from now until next week.

"Uh huh. The one audition training session that I did, I divided everything up into the one's, two's and three's. I had one as 'Very Confident', two as 'In Progress' and three as 'Challenging'. The second category would be the most lengthy, but I put a good number in the first. There are still a few problems with a couple of those. If I'm very confident about them but I can't play them in my sleep...?"

Then they go in with the two's.

"It's funny, I wound up having another category between one and two. Maybe I could use that as the repository for the ones that I'm very confident about but that still have a glitch or two. So that could be 1A. Those are close but not quite. And then the two's would be ones that I definitely can't play the first time and feel confident, and the three's are the ones I'm having difficulty with."

Challenging.

"Yeah, challenging. Well, I think that I say that because I figure I should be able to play all of them."

Do you know anything about centering?

"I know something about it. Basically just try to clear your mind of all other extraneous thoughts. Let them flit about, but don't give them any real power and just focus on what you really need to focus on, which for me would be what I want to come out of the horn."

OK.

"Instead of worrying about shaking or not getting a good breath, I should think about the next note I want to play and focus on that as much as I can."

Let me describe a step-by step process that you can start to practice and use.

"So this is a step-by step routine?"

Yes. But it takes a minimum amount of time. Basically, you're going to take three deep breaths and simultaneously engage in three different mental processes. With the first breath, on the inhale, you think about a full and deep breath.

"OK. I'm going to write this down. OK, on the first breath..."

On the inhale, breathe slowly in through your nose, and pay attention only to your breath.

"OK, so on the first breath, inhale fully, focus only on..."

Getting a good breath.

"Good intake. OK."

On the exhale, let out all the muscle tension. Drop the energy and make your arms, shoulders or neck feel very heavy or loose.

"OK, focus on relaxation..."

Letting all the tension out with the breath going out.

"Release of tension. OK, that's on the exhale."

On the next breath, be at your center. And this gets a little bit esoteric, but it simply means your center of mass or center of gravity. It's two inches below your navel and two inches into your body, toward your backbone.

"I'll try and visualize that."

Or actually while you practice, put your hand there and try and bring your mind down there. Get out of your head and into your center.

"Yeah, I've heard this. The yoga books I've read mention it, that's it's supposed to be the center. Because when the yogis were breathing it seems that everything is focused there. OK, so on the second breath inhale and exhale?"

Yes, but focus on being at your center. On your third breath, on the intake, say a positive word or phrase, a process cue that captures your best playing. Something a teacher would say to you that's really positive about performing your best, but not necessarily something technical.

"The one I'm using right now is 'relaxed and confident'. How's that?"

That's OK, but the relaxed part is going to come with the first breath. Let me give you an example and then ask you to find a better one. Maybe something like "flowing "or "smooth "or "pure"? I don't know.

"So it would be one or two words that are positive. One that did work for me was 'seamless'."

There you go.

"This was for a specific problem I was having. I was putting a gap between notes in a particular passage, so I just focused on 'seamless' and did the same thing. It came out right. And there are others I can use."

Find one for the next week and use it.

"Exclusively?"

What I don't want you to do is be sitting there, searching for it when you're in the process. Come up with one and try it out several times, and either use it or find a better one and use that one.

"OK. And the positive statement should be about what?"

About how you play your best or whatever word captures what you need do to play your best.

"OK. And this is on the intake of the third breath?"

Yes. And while you're doing these first two-and-a-half breaths, try to look at a nondescript spot on the floor and defocus your eyes or just close them.

"Closed eyes works better for me, at least now."

Then, on the exhale of this third breath, open your eyes and turn your focus or energy out. Direct your full attention to a specific point on the stage as you focus your energy out, like, "Here it comes!". You're not going to actually say it but think it to yourself.

"Like extending Ki or Chi?"

Exactly!

"Alright. So this is something I could do anytime?"

Practice it several times in the next few days. Whenever you feel a lot of nervousness come on, let this be your response. When you're doing your audition prep excerpts, you can use it right before you go in. After a few days, you'll get comfortable with it. Then put some extra pressure on yourself and use it to play well.

"I practice for a few days in neutral and then crank it up? So I'll be starting that kind of practice before I talk to you next?"

Right. Imagine yourself playing in a tough situation or an audition or take out one of your pieces and have this be your response to it.

"Or I could try and get the physical manifestation going by running in place and seeing if I can get my heart beats down and get relaxed, because that's often what it feels like."

Now we're talking. That's it. Try to induce the physical reaction, then use the centering to deal with it.

"OK. I will practice that. It will be a good way to start before every practice session or rehearsal. I've got a rehearsal tomorrow morning, so I'll go over this a few times. I'm playing first horn unassisted on the Britten *War Requiem* and of course, I want to do well. That will be a pressure situation."

So play with it today and find a way that will start to work for you.

"And that's it?"

Well, we're going to refine and develop it, but...

"So what you want me to do is practice this...."

...and commit to doing your diary and your routine.

"Commit to a practice routine. Yeah. I made a good start on that yesterday and today."

Good, keep it going. Can we talk Monday?

"Yes. I've got a rehearsal in Hamilton and will be getting back around 11:00. How about if I call you at 11:30? I should be back by then."

That's 8:30 my time. That's good.

"I'll let you know about all this and hopefully I'll be prepared to read you my practice routine."

Super!

"This is the kind of motivation I needed, a little push. Thanks."

You're welcome, Brian. Take care and I'll talk to you Monday. Have a good week.

"You too. Bye now."

CHAPTER FOUR

VERONICA, THREE DAYS AFTER OUR LAST CALL. I want to go back to my notes of our last conversation. Let's start with the breathing. Tell me about how it went.

"Well, it was pretty good. I liked doing it. With about half of them, I wasn't thinking of other things. But I can't say that I ever completely left the external surroundings."

This isn't supposed to be an out of body experience.

"Oh...OK." (laughs)

But it is supposed to get you less distracted or less concerned with outside things, and more focused on one point.

"I would say that I definitely did that four or five times and then thoughts would creep in."

Good. Was it arduous?

"No, no."

We're going to build on that then. I first needed to see whether that was unpleasant, uncomfortable or impossible for you to do.

"No, it wasn't."

And it sounds like you could do it.

"Oh yeah!"

Then you just need to practice it a little bit more for the next few days. So that's good; that's step one. Did you feel, for those four or five times, that you actually got out of your head and down to your center?

"Uh....yeah.....I think I got a little piece of that."

Well, since this is your first experience with it, you're off to a good start.

"Oh good."

Did you come up with the cue words for those four pieces?

"Yeah, I did. I hope I did it right. One word is the same in all of them. Is that OK?"

We'll see. Take me through them one at a time.

"For the serious Rossini piece, I wrote down that when I'm singing it best I feel 'calm' and 'connected' and my voice is 'steady throughout', like I don't get over-excited at any one place. When I'm singing it, I feel like I'm alone and I become unaware of people listening."

We're going to need to get to that one, because that pertains not just to these pieces, but to your inside-out focus. That's fantastic!

"Oh good."

And the other Rossini piece?

"I think about 'words' or 'text' and also 'calm' or 'in control' and that same feeling of being alone."

OK. What do you mean by "in control"?

"Well, the piece has a lot of fast singing in it, yet I never feel like it's a runaway train. I'm still singing every note, even though it's really fast."

And when you do that, it's good?

"Yes."

And you're able to do that?

"Sometimes."

Wonderful! So pick either "'words "or "text. " Which one would it be?

"Oh...'words'."

So there are two good ones, "words "and "in control". Super. Then the *Carmen*?

"OK. I don't know if it makes sense, but when I'm singing it very powerfully or speak strong and really simply, I'm not doing anything too much, and I'm calm."

"Strong"and "simple?"

"Yes. And the last one was Bernstein. And I'm 'absorbed' in it and 'connected'. That's all I could come up with. But I used 'connected' already."

That's not a problem. But as opposed to the other three pieces, this one doesn't sound like you're as far along and committed as the others. It still sounds like you're searching a little bit.

"Well, it's funny...because it's the easiest one to connect with emotionally, but it is hard to sing. But I never have a problem getting absorbed into it. I can get absorbed into it pretty easily and I don't get as distracted when I sing it."

There's the inside-out focus.

"But it is the hardest to sing."

Why?

"Vocally. It has some vocal things that are difficult."

OK. Think about this for a second. Let's say you go to a great teacher or a voice coach that you really respect and say, 'I've got a question for you. This Bernstein piece is difficult. Can you help me with it?' After they listen to you sing it, what would they say for advice to help you get past the difficult part?

"Hmmmm. I guess when I go through the difficult part, they would probably say that I was acting like I was scared of it, so I was cutting off my voice and not singing as well as in the rest of the piece. So I would need to....?"

You're right on track. I'm hearing "scared "and "cutting off your voice." So what is the correction? What would they tell you to do instead of being scared?

"Well, it's like in the *Carmen*...because there was the one place where I came up with 'strong'. When I thought I had to be even more powerful, I was able to get through it."

Aaaahhhhh.

"So it's probably the same thing."

OK. So could we say "absorbed", and "strong" or "powerful"?

"Yeah! That's good!"

We're there. We'll come back to those later.

"OK."

Let's go to the issue of your awareness of other performers, your concerns about the audience and being distracted by outside things. They all go together. Do you buy that?

"Yes!"

Imagine yourself standing on stage. See yourself as the center of a hub, the middle of a wheel, standing in that center.

"OK."

Now there are all sorts of things that can pull you out of that center, whether it's your being aware of somebody watching you, somebody making noise, someone opening a door and coming into the hall, or your being too concerned about the audience. These things will pull you out of your center and put you into an outside-in orientation. But you want to be singing from your center, from inside-out.

"Yeah."

It's like a bicycle wheel with spokes going out. Everything outside tends to pull you out of your center. Instead of seeing that image, see yourself now standing on the stage and being able to get centered and then singing from there. Do you see how that works?

"Yeah."

Hold that thought. Now from that place, you can project your voice out to where you want it to go, rather than be involuntarily pulled by outside things. So you can project your voice out, but you stay at your center.

"That's hard to do because you have to trust that your voice is actually going to get out there, without jumping up and down and screaming."

So you need to trust that your voice will get out there?

"Yes. Without doing extra things."

Such as...?

"Like, I think I sometimes do things with my body. I'll stick my head out sometimes, or take a step or just have a general posture that's leaning forward. Just a further assurance that I'll get out there, but it never helps."

Singing from your center is very powerful and it's one of the most helpful things you can do in performances and auditions.

"Oh yeah, my audition..."

Tell me again about the audition.

"It's in Chicago, I leave a week from today and the audition is a week from tomorrow. It's for the Lyric Opera of Chicago Young Artists Program and it's the final round."

So you've already been through some of the others? How did they go?

"OK.....uh......let's just say they were OK auditions. I guess they were obviously good enough to get to this round, but they weren't the best."

How many people are trying out?

"There are about twenty. I don't know how many positions there are. I assume they'll hire four to six people."

Well, I'll give you a few more things to do right now and then we're going to make sure that they work. I'd like to talk with you early next week and check on how you're doing.

"That sounds good."

When you're not singing well, what muscles or parts of your body are tight?

"When I'm not singing well, usually I have all kinds of neck and jaw tension, and I can't get my abdominal muscles to make any difference in my singing. I just can't, no matter how much I try."

Because they're too tight?

"Yeah. Because it doesn't matter how much air I can push up. It's just not connected. And if my jaw's too tight, it's not going to get through. It's like being very uncoordinated."

And when you're singing well, your neck, jaw and stomach are all....what?

"They're all working but they're much more flexible and my posture's better."

When you were doing your breathing, did you feel that you could just as easily do it sitting up?

"I think I could."

OK. Take the breathing from laying down to doing it sitting up, but certainly with good posture.

"OK."

Then you'll be taking nine good breaths. The first three breaths, as you breathe in, pay attention to your abdominals and getting a good breath. It might help when your doing this to close your eyes. On the exhale, consciously relax your neck and jaw for three breaths. So on your inhale for those breaths, you're working on your stomach. On the exhale, you're working on being flexible and relaxing your jaw and neck. I'm not talking about getting sloppy and loose and letting your head fall, but finding the right level and being relatively relaxed. So does that make sense?

"Yes."

For the next three breaths, be at your center. Think of it as your base. It's a very powerful place to sing from. That's where martial artists, like in karate and aikido, fight from.

"Oh, really? Hmmmm....."

Yeah. They don't fight from their head. They fight from their center. I want you to see it as a source of your power and energy. What you're doing is getting in touch with that.

"OK."

Now, on the last sequence of three breaths, go back to your cue words. Start with the serious Rossini, and on the first two breaths, say your cue words to yourself.

"Alright. In my head?"

Yes. So you're still paying attention to your abdominals and saying "calm and "connected" for those two breaths.

"Right."

But say them with conviction. Don't just go through the motions. Really get in touch with what they feel like and mean. Make them powerful for you.

"Right."

On the inhale of the third breath, get in touch with your center.

On the exhale, open your eyes and narrow your focus to a point someplace in front of you. Then, from your center, project that energy out to that point. Are we OK so far?

"Uh huh."

Do this sequence until you have it memorized and it flows. Practice it five or ten times until you're comfortable with it. Then try it with the *Carmen* and the other Rossini piece, using their cue words.

"OK."

After you get the mechanics down, sing the first few bars, projecting your energy from your center to that point through your voice.

"Ahhhhhhhh. OK."

I don't know how many notes that is, maybe thirty seconds from the beginning of each piece. Because right now, our focus is on getting each of these started correctly. And after you do that, you're on cruise control. The words will cue you to remember what you need to do to sing well.

"So, once I get this sequence of breaths and everything down, I should start to sing right away?"

Yes, do that for the first piece and then leave the room. Get a drink of water or do something else before you start the centering sequence for the next one. Make each of them a separate event.

"OK."

This isn't what you'll necessarily be doing before an audition, but we're going through a learning progression first. Ultimately, it will be less than nine breaths and the cue words may change. In fact, by the next time we talk, things may start changing.

"Great."

So that's it for now. I'd like you to practice this several times a day. And then next time we talk, we can make refinements based upon your experiences and your feedback. And then we can start to work on the Bernstein.

"Oh... great." (laughs)

But by then, this technique will be in place and it can help you with it.

"Oh good."

When would you like to talk again?

"How's Monday?"

Super. Around 7:00 in the evening, my time? Or is 10:00 your time too late for you?

"No, no. But I have an audition that evening around 8:45."

Really?

"Yeah, but it's not an important one."

That's wonderful. Do you know what you're going to be singing?

"I haven't picked yet. But I figured that I would choose one that was challenging."

If that's the case, can we talk Monday morning?

"Sure."

We can take the next step and then apply it Monday night at the audition. How many pieces?

"Just two, but I choose what I start with."

Please come up with cue words for those.

"Well, it will be the same ones that I already have."

OK. Well, we're right on track.

"Great!"

Take care.

"Thanks. Good bye, Don."

ൠ

BRIAN, ONE WEEK LATER. "Hi, Don. How are you?"

Fine. How's it going with you?

"Well, it's been a very interesting week. I did a lot of the centering. I practiced it quite a bit. I used it and I had two very good Britten *War Requiems*. I got a lot of compliments and I played very well. So I practiced it and I got to use it under pressure. I still need to work more on being able to relax over the entire length of a concert, because I still wind up feeling tension and not having the tools, either physically or mentally, to stay relaxed. There's a gradual creeping in of tension even as I try to let it out."

OK.

"And I got more opportunities to try it out because the principal's chops have really been in bad shape. He still has that rash, so I may well have to play the whole concert. We have four runouts in a row and Shostakovich's Fifth Symphony has a very big horn part. I've been playing the big solos, the ones that I thought would get me scared. They probably will a little, but I'm prepared to play them and I told the principal that if he needs me, I'll be there. I'm looking at it as an opportunity."

It really is.

"More than likely, probably Wednesday, I'll be playing first on the Shostakovich, so I'll just keep working on these things."

Well, talk me through it.

"OK. Sometimes I'd start out a session with it, sometimes in the middle. Often I'd do it at the end and a couple of times during the rehearsal, and then in the concert. The way my sinuses are right now, I usually breathe through my mouth, for intake and exhale. I wound up breathing in probably faster than you would want. I wasn't just trying to get that wisp of air in. I was pretty much breathing as if I were taking an exaggerated breath for the horn, slower than I would normally and probably a little more fully, but still focusing on good intake. Then I would hold it for just a fraction and let it out, and focus on my shoulders and neck especially. And then on the second one, my inhale and exhale would be both visualizing the center point. I remember that when I really get into the groove and get centered, I get this ticklish feeling right about where you describe the center would be, and get that kind of half-smile and sense of contentment."

That's great!

"I would visualize it and focus on it as much as I could. For the third breath, I wouldn't close my eyes, especially on stage or rehearsal.

I would focus on the back of the hall, where I ought to project, and my positive statement was usually 'warm air' or 'confidence' or 'projection'."

OK.

"And then on the exhale, I would imagine my sound going out. So, specifically for my purposes right now, I can't do any better than that."

Brian, that sounds really good!

"And it worked. I don't have enough tools, like I said. There are times in the Britten concert where we really have to sit there for a time while the chamber orchestra plays, and I could not get comfortable. I didn't fidget, but I could feel my back and shoulders getting a little more tense, and every once in a while I would try to stretch out a little. You know, you can't do too much on stage. If I'd had my druthers, I would have put my horn down and climbed out of my chair and stretched it out, but you can't do that. (laughs) That's what I would have done if I'd been home. But I was able to keep excess tension from creeping in and I did some very good playing."

Good for you.

"So that's definitely a step forward. That's how I look at it."

Boy, you've already refined it.

"Yeah. You probably didn't give me too many specifics on purpose."

You've just taught me some things. Well, that's a lot of good progress. Keep on using it and refining it and finding the best way for it to work for you.

"OK, so keep practicing that everyday."

Yes. And when you're on stage, use it. The ideal situation would be to flood you with extra pressure and then use centering as an ally.

"This week is going to be unbelievable if I have to sit in and play that Shostakovich because it's got a lot of things that I have difficulty with, or have had in the past. I've spent the last few days making a breakthrough. I've gone through some old notes from my teacher in

Chicago. I've been doing something slightly wrong for many years and I just corrected it. It's taken pretty quickly and all of a sudden I've got a lot more ability to play in the soft dynamics. I've made my articulations more of what I want. At my stage, that's a major break-through, actually. So I feel a little less anxiety about the Shostakovich because there are a lot of soft entrances that are solo. I hate to bol-locks those up."

Can you see yourself playing this piece well?

"Actually I can, but I haven't been working on that specifically. What I've been doing is having the music in front of me and saying, 'OK, here it is', and then taking a breath, playing it and feeling com-fortable with it and being confident that it's going to come out like I want. That's the kind of practicing I've done. I hadn't been actually sitting here saying, 'OK, imagine you're on stage and it's the concert'. I haven't really been doing that."

Could you do that a few minutes a day?

"So visualize pressure situations and apply the centering tech-niques?"

Yes. See yourself getting to a much better place, with a half-smile on your face, prepared to play it well, and then see yourself nailing it.

"So see a positive result. This is something I can do at home."

When's your first night with the Shostakovich?

"The first performance will be Thursday night."

And the first rehearsal?

"Wednesday morning. I play it Thursday, Friday and Saturday on the road and then Sunday we play it here for a Contributor's con-cert."

I'd love to talk with you Thursday after rehearsal. You know, last time you mentioned something about your lips.

"I didn't write that down."

I didn't either, but I recall that you said that you feel tension there sometimes.

"Yeah. I've pretty much solved that. It's kind of technical. I had forgotten to set my embouchure on relaxed chops and then I was applying even more pressure and tensing. So I remembered to form a more relaxed embouchure that gives you more "meat" around the mouthpiece. And with my full lips that's a distinct advantage. That's really helped."

Good.

"We had a rehearsal tonight at Hamilton college. It's one of the better halls in this entire region. It's a great place. So I stuck around afterwards and played a few things for a good friend and everything came out great. Just using this technique makes things a lot easier."

I'm glad.

"I certainly have a lot more confidence. I'm able to do more of what I want. I had a physical impediment and I've taken a pretty big step in eliminating it. All that stuff has just happened in the last three or four days."

OK. The other note I had was that you talked about some problems that lead to a lack of motivation. I'm just not hearing that now.

"Yeah. That was the case back then. It's funny...when you find a new way of playing things or get rid of an old problem that's been dogging you for years, that tends to get your motivation going. And with the Shostakovich, that's certainly got me going. But I have to bring my level up a little or I'm not going to play this well. I still do have an old problem that when I see something loud, I use way too much tension. I use more energy than I ought to and I try and play too loud rather than just trusting that I'll project fine. I overdo it."

Maybe that comes back to our centering third breath and perhaps finding a better cue. You said "projection" or "warm air".

"I'm not sure that covers it."

So maybe for the Shostakovich, use a different one for your final cue. And I certainly don't know what that is, but I'm sure you can find one so you don't overdo it

"How about 'float'?"

Something like that.

"Yeah. I just thought of that. It should just 'float' out. I'm using way too much tension and what it does is bind me up. I can't be as flexible as I need to be and my air is locked up. I can feel my stomach muscles, which you're not supposed to."

So does "float" capture all that?

"Uh, no. But it's a good start. You 'float' the sound out because that's a sense of ease, as opposed to hammering the sound out, which is what I have a tendency to do. I could probably come up with a couple of good ones, but 'float' is a good start."

Brian, this is a great opportunity to adapt it to the situation and watch it work for you. And also to use the visualization ahead of time to set that up; to preset that in your mind.

"OK. So before the rehearsal, I should visualize. And tomorrow's practice could set me up pretty nicely, I imagine."

Try to go through it before you even get there.

"Yeah, but tomorrow I have the day off until the concert tomorrow night. That's the one in Hamilton. But I have the whole day of practicing to prepare myself."

Go through it in your mind first, then physically go through it. Put yourself in a situation and then actually play it.

"OK. And imagine myself there on stage and having to play the solo maybe twice and saying to myself, 'I'm going to play it even better this time'. How's that?"

There you go.

"That kind of positive approach, rather than saying, 'Oh, shit! I'm going to screw it up this time'. You know, I also used that Bob thing. The Britten had gone so well on Friday and there's one place where we come in cold, and I'm the lead voice on that. And out of nowhere, I heard Bob starting to rumble, saying, 'Oh boy, you got that yesterday, but what if you miss it today and splatter all over the place?' So I told him to just back off."

Alright! Good for you!

"Didn't miss it."

That's great, Brian.

"So he just kind of shut up. It's funny, he shifted. He was over on the left side this time instead of the right side."

He just wanted to keep your attention.

"So I told him, 'Look. It ain't gonna happen Bob', and it didn't. It was a little closer than I would have cared for though, because he was still hanging on. He almost tried to knock the mouthpiece off or something, but I didn't let him."

Well, he's not going to go away easily.

"No, I don't expect that. Bob's going to be there for a while. He'll pop up when I least expect it."

But that's OK, as long as you have a strategy.

"And it's worked, the two times it's come up. It hasn't happened very often, which is really an improvement. I'm just focusing on playing as well as I can, rather than 'what if'. So I could do myself a world of good by doing some mental training tomorrow."

You could imagine yourself in a pressure situation or even do something physical to mimic how you'd be feeling and then center before you actually play one of the pieces.

"Maybe do something like run in place and get myself all pumped up, or make myself really nervous."

And trust that the centering will get you where you need to be to play well.

"Yeah, that will give me something to do tomorrow. My training diary has been off and on. I am at least keeping track of my practice everyday. But some of these late nights, the last thing I've wanted to do is come home and write stuff."

I'm sure.

"But I do remember things. I know that I'm telling you more than I've written in the training diary, but it's very uppermost on my mind. I just looked through the notes because we talked about getting my practice routine better established. This is something I've wanted to do; I've got all these good notes and stuff and I'm not using them, so I've started going through them and I picked this up and thought, 'I remember that. I should try this'. And it was like...Bing!"

Ahhhh. Isn't it wild the way that works?

"Yeah. It finally took twelve years to finally sink in completely. It had sunk in to some extent, and I was close at times, but I'd always fall back on my old habits."

It's easy to do. But it sounds like you're doing much better. Let's figure out a time to talk again.

"OK, do you want me to call you Thursday night after rehearsal?"

Actually, I would love to talk to you Friday morning.

"Oh, so after the first performance?"

Yeah. How does that sound?

"Alright, I'll call you at 11:00 and let you know how well it went."

Hey, now we're talking!

"I feel that this has been a big burden off me because I think I've finally figured out something that's been holding me back. I know that there has been some impediment and it isn't just mental. There's a physical component to it too."

There usually is.

"Yeah. It's just an old habit. This may not be the absolute cure for everything, but I honestly think that I'm not a "mouthpiece of the week" person. I don't think that the horn is holding me back, although this new Berg horn certainly has been an improvement over the old Schmidt. But I always go back to me. (laughs) Not the instrument, not everybody around me, but this had been holding me back and I think I've discovered a good chunk of it, if not most of it."

That's great.

"And I'll just continue to work on it and see what happens. You know, I've got to do it. I mean, the principal horn is counting on me. He'll be sitting right next to me playing assistant so we'll make it a team effort. He knows my weaknesses and he'll help me through it."

I have faith in you.

"Thanks. I think it's going to go just fine. But I won't leave anything to chance. I've been working over some of the entrances that I think are going to be a little scary or I'm not confident about. I've been trying to use more of my right brain and what I want to create and go by sound; sound is the primary criterion. All I have to do is hear that high G and play it and it's coming out well just about every damn time."

Oh, that's great.

"Now I guess my task is to make sure that once I'm in the rehearsal situation, I don't revert to my old habits."

Yes.

"And once the rehearsals are going, I'll build on those to make sure that, when it's the concert, I'm just going to continue to do the same things. I'll be more nervous. A concert is always more anxiety, more nerves, more adrenalin. Not all of that is bad, it gets me more pumped up. But there is more opportunity for getting too much adrenalin."

Well then, just go back to centering.

"So I can use tomorrow to practice for the rehearsal and the rehearsals to practice for the concert."

And use the concert to practice for...

"The audition!"

Exactly.

"I just need to keep at it."

I like what I'm hearing.

"Good!"

I'm going to try and get that Shostakovich piece so I know what you're playing.

"Oh, there are so many recordings. It really is a war horse. One of the more popular ones, because it's such a great piece."

Well, good. I'll look forward to hearing it.

"I'll try to get a broadcast. If I'm playing first on it and I have as good a performance as I think I'm going to have, that will be a keeper and I'll send it to you."

I'd enjoy that. Thanks. Well, Brian, it seems like you're right on track.

"OK, well you just keep steering me in the right direction."

I will. And I'll look forward to Friday.

"Alright, thanks. You take care."

You too. Bye bye.

CHAPTER FIVE

VERONICA, A WEEK AFTER OUR LAST CONVERSATION. So...bring me up to date.

"OK. I did the new addition to the breathing exercises, but it was hard to do. We talked about saying the words during breathing..."

...with meaning and conviction.

"Right. I couldn't say them all with conviction and I couldn't immediately go to sitting up and doing it. I had to lay down to do it for a while. But then I started getting better and better."

That's the practice.

"Yeah. So that went well. So...what else? I didn't have time to begin singing the first part of each piece. I had time to do it with only one song. But what was interesting was the way that I would sing it with the cue words. It would be the way that I would sing it when I'm practicing. Maybe having the cue words will help me to do the same thing in an audition. I always wondered, 'How come I have the courage to sing it like this by myself, but I never have the courage to sing it this way in an audition?' Why is that?"

Ahhhhhhhh! Good question. Tell me more about that.

"Well, because during difficult vocal sections, you can't back away from it. There is a chance that you can crash and burn, but pulling away from it is not going to make it any better. It's just going to make it very weak."

Yes.

"But when I'm practicing, there's absolutely nothing at stake so I can be vulnerable and risk making a big mistake because I'm by myself. But in auditions, I won't be able to do that extra-strong thing, particularly in this one. I'm talking about the *Carmen,* where you just have to do it. You just have to have a lot of strength singing it. The end part's very difficult."

Wait, wait. Let me write that down. *Carmen*...end part difficult. Good. We will come back to this. Tell me more.

"Well, I had to change my cue words on one song."

To what?

"Can I use the word 'focus'?"

On which one?

"On the lighter Rossini. 'Words' just didn't do it for me."

Good. You're finding cues that you can say with meaning and conviction, not sarcastically.

"Yeah, right, right. So instead of 'in control', I just used 'control', and that worked."

Wonderful! You're moving along. What else?

"Ummmm......I'm trying to get a better sensation of where my center is... definitely... definitely...and being able to visualize it. And a couple of times when I did the breathing exercises, when you open your eyes and project your voice out to a place, I was able to get the sensation of what that actually feels like; being able to do that and stay strong in my position."

And what's that feel like?

"Ummm.....really good. It feels really solid."

Ahhhhh. You're doing just great!

"And I've decided that I'm going to sing the lighter Rossini tonight and this weekend."

Perfect! Well, let's work today on just the light Rossini. Let it be a trial run-through, so you can get things working for you. So on the light Rossini, tell me the cue words again.

"They're 'focus' and 'control'."

Define what you mean by 'control'.

"Ummm, basically I mean breath control; that I'm supporting every note I'm singing and that I'm keeping a steady tempo.

Otherwise things can get very ugly."

(both laugh)

"Plus it keeps me holding myself back that way in this piece. It makes me take the time I need with the music and with what's going on."

The holding yourself back?

"Yeah. I suppose that wouldn't be great for everybody, but since I get very over-excited and want to run up and sing it...."

So holding back makes you more what?

"Umm...more calm."

Is there anything else I should know before we start?

"Oh, oh. I don't know! I don't think so!" (laughs)

Here we go then. When you're either sitting down or laying down and you take your nine breaths, do the first three breaths help your muscles to relax?

"When I'm thinking about it, yes."

Well, when you're doing the three breaths, are you thinking about it?

"When I'm thinking 'inhale', I think about my abdomen and then on the exhale, I relax my neck and jaw. I realized how tense it was before I relaxed it."

OK, then I want you to continue doing that on the first three breaths. On the next three, when you visualize being at your center, are you getting a better feel for being there?

"Ahhh........I think so. Yeah. I usually visualize being at my center and also feel it at the same time. Is that OK?"

Do you feel like that's getting you out of your head and more focused on one point?

"Yes, definitely. Oh, and I can do it sitting up now."

Hallelujah! Way to go, Veronica!

"Thanks."

OK. In terms of preparing for tonight's audition, would you like to stay with sitting down as opposed to standing?

"Umm...it doesn't matter. I mean, I can try it either way."

So today, you could practice centering while you're standing and also try to cut back on the total number of breaths from nine to six.

"Oh...but tonight before the audition...?"

Tonight, as long as they have a chair there, you could do it sitting down. I'm not recommending that you lay down.

"I've seen weirder things at auditions." (laughs)

Whatever feels comfortable to you. I'm fine with your sitting. And for tonight, if you need to take more breaths, please do so, so that you accomplish what you need in each sequence.

"OK."

If you go there and it takes you four or five breaths to get your jaw relaxed, well then, take more.

"Oh, OK."

But stay there until you've accomplished it. And then the same thing with your center. If, because of stuff going on around you, it takes more than three breaths, then take more and stay there until you get there.

"I see."

The purpose of this is to make it work for you; it's not just to do a drill.

"Right, right."

So during the third sequence, on the first couple of breaths, think 'control', and everything that it means to you. And then when you've got a good sense for 'control', then move to 'focus'. And with that focus from your center, open your eyes and project it out through your voice to a point. Does that work for you?

"Yes. Yeah."

Now today, do that with the light Rossini and sing the entire aria.

"OK."

Oh...I've got something else for you to do. You've got to trust me on this one. The reason why we're doing this is because you're going to feel some anxiety before you sing. I promise.

"Oh God."

(both laugh)

Here's the drill. I hope you like this. (laughs)

"Oh, my God. OK....."

Do you live in an apartment?

"Yeah."

What floor?

"Third."

Ahhh, that's perfect. I would literally like you to set up a tape recorder, turn it on, leave your apartment and run up and down the stairs to get your heart going.

"OK."

I'm not saying ten minutes, I'm just saying get your heart really going.

"In any way that I want?"

Any way that you want to do it. Then come back into the room with the tape recorder already going, and while your heart's still pumping, get centered and then sing the light Rossini all the way through.

"Ooooooh......oh God! OK. Let's see if I can calm myself down, basically."

Well, here's the thing, Veronica. Centering is a great, great tool and you need to see how good it is and to learn to trust it. It's not going to drop your heart rate down dramatically, but it will help. And besides, we don't want to take away all the energy that you could put into your voice.

"Right."

So we're not going to wipe it out. We're just going make it more under your control. Start to practice having it work for you. So today, get your heart rate up, use the centering to get you to a better place and then sing your best. That's the drill.

"OK."

I want you to start using it so you can feel it work. Tonight at the audition, you won't have to run up and down the stairs to get your heart going. (laughs)

"No, it'll probably just be there. Besides, I don't want to get my clothes all sweaty."

Let's go back to your courage. If we took it on a scale from one to ten, with one being very frightened and ten being extremely courageous, would you say that at home, you can sing that at a nine or a ten?

"Uh.....yeah, I can."

And what are you normally in performance situations?

"Probably around a five."

I wouldn't ask you to sing it in public right now at a nine or a ten, but what about a seven?

"Hmmmmmm.....yeah. Yeah, seven would be something. If I sang it at a seven at an audition, I would be proud of myself."

When you're practicing today at home, with the tape recorder on, sing it at an eight and see what it sounds like.

"OK.......alright."

Then tonight, cut it back a notch and sing it at a seven. I'm not asking you to sing it at a nine or a ten at the audition, but a five is more dangerous than a ten. (laughs)

"Yeah. I hate five. Five is just wimpy."

Being over-cautious is no help. You are going to be exposed out there. You might as well let it out.

"OK."

So I want you also playing with that today. Try and get to an eight and watch what it does and then cut it back for tonight.

"So I'm just going to work on the lighter Rossini today. I'll practice the centering and take the amount of breaths I need."

Make it work for you. Can we talk tomorrow morning?

"Yeah, fine."

I'll want to hear how it went and I'll have a few other things for you to do.

"I'm sure you will!"

(both laugh)

"Alright. I'm excited. I can't wait to sing tonight."

Enjoy it and I'll talk to you tomorrow.
"OK, Don. Thanks so much."
You're welcome. Good bye.
"Bye bye."

᠊ᡕ᠊

Brian called about a week later, but I didn't get it on tape. He told me that the Shostakovich went well. He had used the three centering breaths and it worked. He said that he was even considering volunteering to play the Shostakovich again that evening. We agreed to talk the following week. I asked him to practice condensing the number of breaths he took in order to center. He was on his way to a long road trip. He called the following Monday. It was our fifth phone conversation.

"Hi, Don. Is this a good time for you?"

This is a great time. I'm glad we hooked up.

"Yeah. We've managed to keep doing that. So, I think you'd be pretty proud of me. I played the long road gig and played very well. A very hot, dry stage, and I still had a good one. And then the big test, I thought, was yesterday. It was a home concert. I was a little more apprehensive than I had been for the road concerts. I had written down in my training diary, 'Am I going to screw up this time?'. I thought maybe it was because I was home and here it was the fourth one."

But you didn't.

"And another thing that I've noticed about me is that when it's a big hall and you can see the balconies, I have a thing about 'peering eyes'. Like all the tension's focused on me, as unrealistic as that might be most of the time, except during that big solo, then everybody knows who's really playing. So that got me a little more anxious, but I did all my focusing and everything and I played really well. The brass section got bows every concert. But the conductor gave me the first solo bow and the crowd just exploded."

That's great!

"And so did the orchestra. So I felt really good about that."

Good for you.

"So it was a successful, eye-opening excursion. I was actually starting to enjoy it most of the time."

Aren't you supposed to enjoy it?

"Yeah, but not always. It's easy to enjoy on fourth horn when there's less pressure."

So please bring me up to date about condensing the three breaths, and what kind of results you had.

"Yeah, I was able to do it right before the solo this time, when I was a little more anxious. I had been practicing with just one breath in, focusing and then putting my Ki out. It wasn't totally successful, but it was pretty good. It steadied me down enough. I found that when I've got a long stretch and then a solo entrance coming up, if I just concentrate on my breathing and listen to what's being played, rather than thinking, 'Here it comes, 20 bars away', and getting that feeling of impending doom, I do much better. It's not that bad, but it's anxiety, certainly. I would focus on my breathing and sometimes it was difficult to do, but I kept with it. I used to get what I'm sure was the onset of an anxiety attack, and I felt dizzy, like I was going to fall off my chair. A little bit of a panic reaction. I felt an inkling of that, but it was very brief and I just stayed with it and said, 'Nope, it's not going to get any worse. Just breathe'. I shouldn't say that I fought it off, instead I just let it 'float' away. I did have a momentary feeling of, 'Oh God, not this old thing again!'. That was right at the beginning and I was able to move it off to the side, out of my way."

That's very good.

"And Bob showed up a couple times and I just told him to go away. Boy, that's really one of the best things. You know, it's like, 'Is this going to be the time you miss that first G fortissimo entrance?'. I told Bob to get out of here and maybe come back some other time. But he's the only one I've dealt with so far. I think I need to name those 'peering eyes'..."

Sounds like a smart idea.

"…because I looked at some old notes and I know I feel more comfortable alone in a dark hall. And yet, in the same hall I feel differently when I know that there are people listening, that there are 'peering eyes' out there and it's really silent and you're making almost the only noise. That's something I think I could put my energy toward dealing with and releasing. Letting it go."

What's a good way to reframe that?

"Mmmmmm. Well, I think that the peering eyes are a form of judge. There's somebody out there who has heard me play and is saying, 'Maybe he's going to screw this one up', or something like that."

So, it's the peering eyes of judges?

"I believe so. And obviously I don't feel that if I'm in the hall alone. It's when it's a concert and not a rehearsal. It's not peering eyes of people on stage with me, it's those in the audience sitting out there. And I think that stems from when I was in my school days at Northwestern. We'd go to hear the Chicago Symphony all the time and listen intently. And of course, they'd rarely miss. So now it's reversed and now I'm on stage. I know there are people out there like me; very attentive and listening for every little mistake. So I think that's where some of my anxiety from peering eyes comes from; reversing that role."

So they're like mirrors?

"That's a good way to put it. Well, maybe not a mirror so much as knowing that those kind of people are out there. I've seen people with binoculars and figure they're watching me. So maybe I need to name that feeling, and hopefully it will be as effective as telling Bob to chill. I should find a good name. Bob works really well because it's short and sounds kind of funny."

Pick some different ones, use two or three.

"So I should come up with two to three names for the peering eyes?"

Yes. Like Fred, Mary and Tom.

"Fred and Ethel. They'd make it a pairing. Fred and Ethel... or Lucy and Desi."

Whatever you want, as long as you deal with them like you've been doing with Bob. It would take the harsh edge off. And besides, they might not even be listening. And then you can forget them.

"OK. So they're watching me. And they're judging, but then I forget about them. I get over the feeling soon after the start, because the first entrance is quite a bit into the piece and there are a number of different emotions, and then I come in with the theme. I did it better and better every night. I didn't miss the first note, even though that's one of the bugaboos. Like, 'What happens when you miss that note?'. Because there are many famous orchestra pieces that start with horn. Those always scared me. It's like, 'Oh God, how do you do that?' That used to happen. I'd feel that everybody was watching and I'd feel the pressure. Not that I'd feel my legs heading for the door, but I would definitely be a little light-headed."

That anxiety was a normal part of your development.

"So feeling extreme anxiety was part of my development?"

Yeah. And you've progressed a lot since then, right?

"Oh, yeah!"

But part of you can still experience an adrenalin rush or quick shot of nervousness in certain circumstances. I can't guarantee that you won't feel that. But you've learned how to deal with that better.

"Definitely."

And you're going to learn even better. But the anxiety shouldn't be completely wiped away; it's not necessarily bad.

"Nerves are OK?"

Once that feeling stops, it's time to retire and move on to something you really care about.

"So that shows that I care?"

Yeah!

"That I want to do a good job. There's never a doubt that I want to do a good job."

Could you think about reframing that shot of nervousness? It could it remind you of the good old days or of all the distance you've come since then.

"Could you explain what you mean by 'reframing'?"

Instead of feeling the anxiety and saying, "Oh, shit! That's just what I felt back then", or, "I hope I don't make a mistake now", it's feeling that anxiety and saying, "Yup, I've learned how to deal with that."

"So when I get that feeling...?"

Don't interpret it as a bad or foreboding thing, but just as a reminder of how far you've progressed since then.

"OK, so when I get that feeling, I interpret it and say, 'There it is, my old friend'. How about that? 'My old friend'. I like that. So I interpret the feeling as my old friend and then acknowledge how far I've come in dealing with him."

Something like that.

"And this can be in conjunction with my breathing. I could be there, centering my breath and thinking, 'Yeah. There's my old friend again. He's still with me, maybe he always will be, but I can control him'. I have proven that time and time again."

And that's what we'll call reframing.

"It's always going to be there. It's a part of me."

Well, it'll be less and less of a consequence. You can't necessarily erase it out of your existence, but you can deal with him and then let it go. Like waving to an acquaintance that's walking on the other side of the street. You just don't have any time for him, so it's just a, 'Hey, how are you doing? See you later' kind of thing.

"And I could do this same kind of thing before these concerts. I haven't been totally worrying about it, but I know where I've had a big piece coming up, I won't be living quite as much. I'll be thinking, 'Maybe I'd better not do this because I've got this concert tonight. I'd better not go for a long bike ride'. Sometimes it bothers me. Certainly I wouldn't go off, not warm up and go take a trip and come back with ten minutes before the concert, but the other extreme would be to sit in the house and practice all day and fret, take a nap and worry about everything that could go wrong. I'm not at that extreme either."

Could you find a balance between those two?

"Yeah, I would like to find a balance. And sometimes I do and sometimes I don't. This was a new experience, but if I'd been playing fourth horn instead, I know it wouldn't produce nearly as much anxiety. But if I had a solo engagement, if I were going to play a Mozart concerto, you'd better believe I'd be even more anxious than I was for the Shostakovich. And I know that's not a bad thing necessarily."

You're making a lot of progress and it's starting to work well for you.

"Yeah. I really like the centering technique. OK, now I'd tentatively like to name the 'peering eyes' Fred and Ethel."

Or you can come up with other ones.

"OK. I'll come up with something good."

Just acknowledge them and say, "Thanks for coming to watch". They're some of your old friends, so realize how far you've already come.

"Right, and it's not going to get me. I'm not going to go screaming off stage or fall off my chair. I know that I can play well with that kind of feeling because I did it four times in a row."

Exactly. And that doesn't guarantee ninety-nine times out of a hundred, or a hundred out of a

hundred, but we'll get to that ninety-six repetitions from now. OK?

"Uh huh. So it was a good week."

Tell me your schedule, Brian.

"Well, I wanted to talk to you about my Houston prep, which I got a good start on today. I really want to firm up Houston. I almost have two hours in today and I'm not done yet. I've been going through my old practice notes and there are technical exercises I need to do; to keep up my trills, my slurs, multiple tongueing...things that I should be doing. I just played through some of the cello suites. My chops, with my confidence and the work that I've been doing, everything's working really well. I want to apply that energy toward the Houston list. And that's not my only chance because San Francisco's coming up, and that's another job I would have a very good shot at. So Houston is not my last chance. I've taken a hard look at it. I definitely want Houston, but if it doesn't happen, I'm not going to kill myself."

Think in terms of preparing yourself the best you can for it.

"Yeah. Maybe you could give me a little impetus or help me with something. I went through about half the list, just went through the excerpts one after the other and they all were going pretty well. A couple of them are still giving me trouble, though. I think I ought to redo my list of one's, two's and three's."

That would be great.

"OK, so redo that. Should I keep it to three, or did you like having that sub-category between one and two?"

Whatever works for you. Either way is fine. It's important to put them in separate categories, but think of the three's in terms of challenges or opportunities.

"Maybe the three's should receive my highest priority right now?"

How about the two's and three's.

"So I don't practice those things I'm already good at. Just play the challenging ones."

And come up with a positive thought for each one of them. Like...

"...I can play this better than anyone."

Exactly. Come up with a word or phrase for each excerpt on your three's list, with the same power that was behind that one.

"So assign a unique word...."

...and in your mind, put a 'post-it' note on each excerpt. So you would put the, "I can play this better than anyone" note on that last piece of music. Then when you think of that piece or when you put it on your music stand, that's what you'll hear and see in your head.

"So when I put that excerpt up and it comes into my visual

range, that 'post-it' note with that phrase or word is just there, Boom! front and center, as if it were attached right there, and then I play whatever that evokes for me."

Try to do that this next week for all the two's and three's.

"And each one of those gets its unique word or phrase?"

Yes. I'd love to go through them with you next time we talk.

"OK, so have the 'post-it's' ready for all the two's and three's for next time. Good! That is exactly what I need! I've even made a list of what I'm going to do in this period. I'm going to put together a tape of all the excerpts in the order that's on the list. That's something that I've been putting off. I need to get the music going. My playing is really good right now, but my prep is what needs work. This project is going to be enough right now, because I've got to play the licks and do a little soul searching to find just the right phrase or word for each of them."

That's great! When can we talk again?

"Next week. Monday is good. How about 7:00?"

Fine.

"OK, I'll call you at 7:00 and have the list. I won't have any concerts to tell you about because I don't have any for a while."

Just put yourself in those situations of playing those pieces in auditions.

"Yeah. Go to the mental movies. I got it. Thanks."

Nice talking to you.

"OK. You too. Bye."

CHAPTER SIX

Veronica, the next morning. "So, I did the audition and it was very interesting. I was able to do everything vocally that I wanted to do."

That's wonderful!

"And I was very courageous. It was very interesting! I was still nervous."

I told you that you would be.

"Yeah, I was still really nervous and it was so strange because usually in an audition I kind of go into another part of my brain and just....I don't know what I do! Yet I didn't do that last night. Part of it was hard because I couldn't act out...I was able to stand in one place and breathe really well and do all the vocal things I wanted to do, but I wasn't able to really act as much."

We haven't talked about acting.

"Right!"

(both laugh)

"But I've never done that. Well, I shouldn't say never, but I've very rarely gone to an audition and been able to sing the way I sing at home. And I feel like I did. And I won five-hundred dollars."

That's great, Veronica! Congratulations!

"Yeah! Thanks."

This is wonderful!

"Yeah!"

So what's the bad news?

"Uh... no bad news. I don't think there is any bad news. I was so nervous and I was going to cancel it. I was really going to cancel it...."

I would have shot you.

"I know you would have! That's why I didn't. (laughs)

I have friends in the Mafia in New York. Do you like your knee caps?

"Oh, no!"

(both laugh)

"So I went. That was a very, very, very good experience."

Was the nervousness down a little?

"Um.......well, I think it would reach the same amount, but it came down when it was time to sing. Once I started singing, it was not an issue. But before that... "

Before you go on, you should get nervous. If you're flat, if you don't get nervous, it's time to look for something else that will be important to you.

"Yeah."

Our goal is not to get rid of your nervousness. It's just to not have it affect your singing. But you're going to feel it.

"Right. Oh, yeah."

And you should feel it.

"Oh, good. Because I thought, 'Oh gee....what's wrong?' I'm still nervous."

What I'd love to do is tie it to your courageousness.

"Yeah. OK."

So what I'd like you to do with that is, when you feel nervous, let that remind you to be courageous. Because you are going to feel nervous.

"Right."

And just say, 'Yup, I've been here before. I've done this before. I'm going to be courageous'. OK?

"OK."

So we're going to tie the nervousness to courageousness. Because you're going to feel that, but the idea is to use your courage to work your way past your fears. Take me back to yesterday and to your running up and down the stairs.

"Yeah, I did that. Ran up and down the stairs, ran around the apartment…"

Did that get your heart going?

"Yeah."

Did that mimic, a little bit, some of what you feel at an audition?

"Yeah, it did. Because at least I got the shallow breathing part. And I think I took about fifteen breaths and then I was ready to sing."

And how did you sing?

"OK! It was OK. I kept stopping, though."

Stopping what?

"Whenever I would do something I didn't like, I would go back and do it again. So I don't know if that really counts, instead of just singing it through. I stopped and fixed things and changed it."

OK. Did we talk about perfection at all?

"Yeah, I think we did. That was one of those first things that we talked about a little bit in the first session."

Oh, yeah. I need to define a term for you, and the term is 'optimal'. I'm not sure what it means to you, but let me explain what it means to athletes, OK?

"Yeah."

Everybody going into a pressure situation, whether it's an audition or the Olympics, is going to feel pressure. That pressure is going to affect them either in a minor way or a major way, but it's going to affect them.

"Right."

Probably 99 out of 100 of them will not do as well under that pressure as they're used to doing in less pressure situations, namely in rehearsals or in practice or at home. It just doesn't work that way. Because they're under pressure, they're not going to be as sharp, as good, as relaxed, or as focused as they're used to being in more relaxed situations. So then we bring in the word 'optimal'. And 'optimal' simply means that, given that they're nervous, given that they're feeling pressure, given that people are watching them, given that they know it's important and there are consequences, they're not going to nail it. The best they'll do is 'optimal', namely as good as they can, given the circumstances.

"I see."

But it's certainly not perfection. The one who wins either the audition or the Olympics is not the person that performed perfectly. That rarely happens, and it's just out of the question. The one who wins either the Olympics or the audition is the one who makes the least number of bad mistakes.

(both laugh)

"Right."

And what we're working on is not getting you to sing perfectly. It's getting you to sing as well as you can given that you're feeling nervous. Does that make sense?

"Yeah."

But we're not striving for perfection, or to get you singing the way you do at home. We're trying to get you to sing as well as you can in an audition. And given how we're going so far, that's going to be better than everyone else.

"Oh, good!"

So that's what we're going to call 'optimal.' We're going to always strive for 'optimal,' never perfection. So when you're feeling nervousness, you'll now have a strategy to use. Yes, you'll still feel nervous, your performance won't be perfect, but it should be your best, given the circumstances, which should be better than everyone else because they don't know this stuff.

"Right."

And before Saturday I'm not going to tell any of them.

"Great!"

(both laugh)

So, when you did do the running and you got your heart rate up and respiration rate up and then went through the breathing, did you feel then that you were at least in a better position, in more control, somewhat calmer, than if you hadn't?

"Yes. At the beginning I don't think I could have started. I mean, I could have started singing, but it would not have been very good. But by the end, I could sing."

Great, because that's what we're going to keep on doing. I hope you like your stairs. (laughs)

"Oh, I need a couple more flights, though. I'll have to go down twice."

Whatever it takes. Go outside or whatever. I'm serious; the key thing is to get your heart rate up. And I don't care how you do it. Just so you get it up. Are you used to taking your heart rate?

"Uh, yeah. I used to do it a lot."

OK. I want you to start doing it. How do you do it?

"Um, let's see. Either 15 seconds or 30 seconds on my wrist."

I want you to keep on doing it. Do you know what your resting heart rate is?

"No. I mean, not now."

OK. Here's what I'm going to ask you to do. I want you to start keeping track of it and certainly get it up to 90 or 100.

"OK."

And then when we start doing audition run-throughs, I'm going to ask you to do it then too, so I just want you to get used to it. But here's where we're going with that. Let's say you run up and down your stairs in your apartment and you get your heart rate to 100. Then you do your breathing and bring it down, and you sing well. Well, then before you go into the audition and you feel your heart pumping, I'm going to want you to feel your pulse and say, 'Yeah, it's100. I've been practicing at 100'.

"Oh, yeah. I see. Oh, good."

Because it's the same.

"Yeah."

And it really doesn't matter whether you get it up from running up and down stairs, or just from walking into an audition. It's the same response and you're going to have the same solution.

"OK. Great!"

So the Rossini piece went well?

"Yeah! Yeah!"

Super. So here's the next thing. Are you ready?

"Yeah."

Let's move to the other pieces and do the same thing.

"OK."

How long are those pieces? How many minutes?

"Oh God...*Carmen* is a little over two minutes. The Rossini is probably four minutes and the Bernstein four minutes as well."

You mean both Rossini pieces are four minutes?

"Yeah. Well, the lighter Rossini is probably a little less, but they're each around four minutes or a little less."

What I'd love for you to do is...is there a place where you can go, like a rehearsal hall or studio where you can just go in and just sing?

"Hmmm....no. I don't think so."

Is there any place outside of your apartment where you sing?

"Just in lessons and with coaches and auditions."

Do you think you could find a place that's convenient?

"That's not in my apartment?"

Yes.

"Yeah, I could at someone else's house. Does that count?"

Yes.

"OK, yeah."

Please check into that because your place is very comforting, it's security. I want to get you out of there, but not for the stuff that we're doing. I want you to keep on practicing there. But I would love you to set up a situation. Let me just give you an example. At a friend's house, at seven o'clock, tell that friend, especially if they're a singer or a musician, that you'd like to come over and go through your songs.

"Ooooooo......"

Yeah.

(both laugh)

"OK. They don't have to watch or anything, do they?"

Not the first night. (laughs) Veronica, I'm going to keep on putting pressure on you because there's nothing I can do about the pressure that's going to be put on you at the audition, other than preparing you for it and teaching you how to deal with it. But listen, you can do it.

"Oh, yeah. Yeah. Alright."

Courage is like a muscle. You strengthen it by using it.

"Oh, I like that."

So I'm just going to raise the bar.

"I'm ready for the next level."

Try to set that up. Not necessarily for tonight but certainly by Wednesday or Thursday.

"OK."

I want you to start bringing the number of breaths down.

"Ahhhh..."

I'm not going to put a number on it, I just want less. But I don't want you leaving any one of the segments until you've done it. In other words, don't move on until your neck and jaw are relaxed. But hopefully, get that to be fewer breaths.

"OK."

And then don't move on until you're really at your center.

"OK."

Did you feel more focused last night?

"Yeah, I did. Well, basically I felt more like I was really in control."

Ahhhhhhh!

"I felt like I'm the one that's deciding how this piece is going to be. Not the piano player. It's me, and I can take my time where I want to take my time."

Wow! That's wonderful!

"Yeah! That's what I felt. Focused? I think I might have to change that because I was using that as one of cue words. I don't know....I think it might be too vague for a cue word."

Good. Keep on refining it.

"Yeah. I'll just find something else."

Yup. And we're going to keep on refining it. These cue words won't be the same for the next twenty years. We're going to use them and eventually they'll wear out. They'll have no meaning to you; you'll just be mouthing the words. And that's when it's time for us to move on. So we'll be continually finding new words. And your singing's going to change. What you need now, you may not need a month from now. You may need something else.

"Wow!"

So always be looking for the right words to take in with you. Plan ahead of time.

"OK."

So in other words, I don't want to be sitting outside the audition thinking, 'Now is it 'control' or is it 'focus' or...?

(both laugh)

So, did you do the breathing sitting or standing before you went in?

"I did it sitting."

OK. I want you to also try to start transitioning to standing.

"OK."

Did you put the tape recorder on yesterday?

"Yeah."

I meant to tell you, I don't necessarily want you listening to it.

"Oh good. I listened to parts of it."

I don't want you chopping it up. But again, that's just another source of pressure.

"Yeah, it is, actually."

Again, I'm going to keep on asking you to take on more pressure and then deal with it. So, more standing than sitting. Fewer breaths as opposed to more. Keep on looking for good cue words. Let me write that down......OK, here's the next step. Have you found good cue words for the Bernstein piece yet?

"Ummm....let's see. Not really."

I want you to, OK?

"OK."

So that's your first assignment. The next one is to get your heart rate up with the tape recorder on, come back in and sing one piece all the way through without stopping.

"OK."

Then do two pieces all the way through without stopping, and then three pieces all the way through without stopping. And that may take you a day or two to get through that, but I want you to go through all three pieces without stopping.

"OK. Oh, wow!"

Yeah, I know. Again, I don't want it to be, 'Well, I'm just at home and nobody's listening, so I can stop'. I want you working through it.

"OK. I have another audition on Thursday night."

Wonderful!

"Ooohhh. So I'll sing another piece."

So that's where we are.

"OK."

And then, after you do the three, I'm going to start asking you to switch them around. But I'm also going to want you to go through the Bernstein piece.

"OK."

Do you know what you're going to be singing at the audition on Thursday night?

"I figured that I'd start with the serious Rossini."

Oh, good. Same pieces then?

"Same pieces exactly."

Good. Can we talk Thursday morning?

"Yeah!"

Good. Because you're doing great.

"I am?"

You're right on track.

"Oh, good."

You've got to trust me. You're really right on track.

"Well, I was so relieved after last night because part of the ner-

vousness was because of this weekend. But you can't ignore these feelings and just hope that they're going to go away."

No, Veronica, they're going to be there.

"Yeah."

They're just not going to affect your performance.

"OK. Good."

But they're going to be there, I promise you.

"Uh huh. Alright. Oh good!" (laughs)

I'm sorry. If you don't want the nervousness, get out of opera.

"I love it, though!"

And that's part of the reason you're nervous. It's because you do
love it and you want to sing well.

"Mmmm mmmmm."

So what's a good time on Thursday morning?

"Is eleven o'clock good?"

It's perfect.

"OK."

Questions?

"Uh...nope. I've got to go to a friend's house and sing, keep
doing that, do what I did with the Rossini yesterday, and do that
with my other pieces. Ooohhh, that's a lot of work. I'll be busy."

Yup. Get the breathing down, do it standing, go through the
pieces with no stopping, and find a friend's house to use.

"OK. I'll do that tomorrow. OK!"

Alright. You just keep up the good work. You're going great!

"I will. Thanks so much, Don."

You're welcome.

"OK. I'll speak to you on Thursday."

Good. Take care, Veronica. Bye bye.

ᔕ

BRIAN. A WEEK LATER. So tell me how it went this past week?

"I've made really good progress on a number of excerpts, including the category three's."

So in terms of practice?

"In terms of practice, it's been an extremely productive week. And in terms of life in general, I got a lot of things done. I got some good bike-riding in, and I'm playing really well."

Did you start using the 'post-it' notes?

"Yeah. I definitely have the list established with the one's, two's and three's. As a matter of fact, I've been shifting a few of them around. I moved one up to the second and one back down to the third, because I was pissed at it. But as far as the mental 'post-it' notes go, were they supposed to be a word or phrase that describes how I feel about the piece or what I want to do with it?"

You can start with whatever first comes to mind with an excerpt.

"So for like the Beethoven's Seventh Allegro excerpt, I just put 'springtime', because it reminds me of springtime. And for the Beethoven Seven Trio, it's a 'relaxed lilt' underneath the nice woodwind melody. But for most of these, I couldn't come up with a very good label. Maybe I missed what you were driving at."

The specific label is not the important thing, it's just a starting point. But especially for the excerpts in the third category, you need to come up with a process cue that captures how you play when you play it well.

"I do have them for almost all of them. Only two aren't named. There are six total in category three. The only thing I don't have named is the Haydn Double Concerto, because I don't know the piece at all. It's in category three because I've never worked on it."

What are some of the words or phrases you have for some of the other three's?

"Well, for the Beethoven Nine I have 'tranquil and confident'. And for Strauss's *Heldenleben*, 'crisp and menacing'. How's that?"

Is that you or the piece?

"Both. There's a certain part of it that should be crisp, and it is menacing. But I found I played an audition round today and I just pulled numbers out of a hat. I wound up playing three of the six category three's on the list and I stunk. No way to play an audition. But I learned a couple of good things. I tried to overplay the one that's crisp and menacing, and that's before I named it. So I'm trying to be crisp and menacing, rather than overpowering with it. Crisp is not like a sledge hammer."

So when you bring that piece out and it captures your attention, the thought of "crisp and menacing" should come to mind.

"And that's the mental 'post-it' note that I will attach to it. Yeah, for the opening of the Mahler First Symphony, I have 'warm, thin air stream'. That's certainly different from 'springtime', or 'crisp and menacing'. Is that more of a process cue or is there no difference between those two?"

They're similar, and both of those are fine.

"The 'relaxed lilt' sets me up to play that well, because one of my teachers said, 'You know, it's a relaxed excerpt. Don't try and blow the crap out of it'. That's sometimes my tendency. For Tchaikowski Four, I have 'rhythmic intensity' because, again, he told me that this is not a lick that you're supposed to blow the crap out of. They want to hear the intensity and the drive out of the rhythm. They want to know that you can stay consistent with the rhythm and know how the tune goes."

Good. Did you come up with any others?

"I think I only have a quarter of them named. Actually, the ones I haven't named in category three are page-long excerpts, and I'm preparing to play the whole page. For the *Don Quixote,* I said 'storm-swept rocks' because it's two excerpts, two variations from *Don Quixote* and one uses a wind machine in back of the percussion. And the other one is a rising and falling melodic line, and I haven't come up with a good name for that yet."

OK.

"For the *Rheingold* excerpt, I came up with 'smooth waves', and I've been working on a glissando technique that a friend of mine told me about. It's a lot better, but it's still going to stay in category three."

How about your centering exercises?

"I've been doing them, and although I haven't had the pressure situations to try it out, I did the full boat. I jogged in place and thought all these negative thoughts, and then calmed myself down and came in and played like crap."

Why was that?

"Because they were excerpts that I wasn't playing well. And it was in the morning, right about the time when I'll be playing, about two weeks from today. But it didn't concern me that much."

So then make sure that you put that into your routine every day.

"As a matter of fact, I have another list. I have a short and a long list that I want to do every day. The long list is more like a semi-finals list."

How are the images in your head of how it's going to go?

"As far as going to the movies about Houston?"

Yes.

"I've not done much of that."

OK.

"I think I'm just about to start, though. I used this last week to kind of get me going, to get a practice routine established and work on the excerpts. I've made progress on a lot of them. Of the excerpts I've played so far, *Fidelio* was perfect and the other Beethoven went pretty well, and the Tchaikowski Fourth was pretty good. I haven't listened to the tape yet. I did it this morning and I let it sit for a while. I taped some other things. So I'm going to come back to that tonight before I do my long list. Yeah, I need to start and I'm going to be playing for a friend on Wednesday, so he'll just run me through my paces."

Super!

"One of my concerns is that I did this before Detroit, playing really well, and then I seemed to ramp down about a week before, in intensity and in playing level. And by the time I got to Detroit, I was definitely in a trough. The way I was for Detroit was the way I was last week. I mean, this last week I was just hot. I was playing every-thing. And I don't quite feel that now, but I do realize what I've done is probably reached another plateau."

OK.

"I think I've reached about three plateaus in the last two months, maybe even month and a half. My playing is really doing that kind of upward spiral. So I might be on another plateau. I'm not going to panic, but I would appreciate the benefit of your experience as far as peaking too early as opposed to peaking at the right time, because I really didn't do something right in Detroit. I felt mentally and emotionally unprepared. If I'd gone in the week before I would have won it, the way I was feeling. I don't want to do that again."

And you've got two weeks to go, right?

"Yeah. Two weeks from today."

Let's work through that together. The idea is to see yourself playing better and better and better.

"Yeah. That definitely has been happening."

And as long as you're not there with all the pieces in category three, just keep on moving forward.

"I've been working on the category three's and giving them a lot of attention."

That's great! And just keep on until they're all category one's.

"I was working on some category two's as well. And I don't want to forget about the one's either!"

Please do all three when you put yourself into the routine.

"So pull some out of each category?"

Yes.

"So what do you think could have caused me to peak early for Detroit and start the downward slide?"

I'm really not interested in dredging that up or setting you up so that happens again. Let's just move forward.

"So there's no preventative maintenance needed to be done as long as I keep progressing?"

That's the idea.

"So, I had set some deadlines for myself to have everything named by Sunday, and to have a tape of all the excerpts; neither of which I did. What I have been doing is some listening, and what I'll do tonight, as soon as we're finished, is play the Beethoven Nine, the entire third movement at least twice, maybe three times. Just sit there in front of the stereo, play with the music, because I've got the whole part. This is just for pacing and just to feel comfortable, because I want to feel as tranquil and relaxed at the end as I did in the beginning. It's a long excerpt and I tend to get tension built up. So if I can do the whole movement a couple of times, whatever excerpt they throw at me, it should be that much easier."

Why don't you do that, and if there's anything other than you nailing it, let's talk about it in a few days.

"The Beethoven in particular?"

Yeah. If there's anything we need to discuss, let's get to it then.

"So what I'll do is treat it as a performance..."

Yes.

"I'll sit there before I cue up the tape and take my three breaths. I hadn't been practicing that as much, because I hadn't been at rehearsals or anything. I've been off."

The other thing you might want to do is figure out some different places to put yourself in performance situations.

"So I should do more mental movies?"

Well, not only more mental movies, but physically do it. I'm not saying you should rent a rehearsal hall, but if you could stay fifteen minutes after a rehearsal or go there half an hour early and put yourself in a different physical circumstance, and put yourself on the spot to play....

"Oh, I see. How about if I'm standing backstage before rehearsal and people are warming up and stuff and I'm doing an excerpt or two. People are always listening. That's somewhat of a pressure situation, because if you screw something up, people are going to hear. People are generally into their own routine, but that's a little bit of pressure."

Yes.

"And then treat that with the same centering techniques?"

Exactly.

"Or I could play backstage during breaks. I do that anyway, but I haven't done that specifically. OK, I'll get there early on Wednesday. We've got a double rehearsal on Thursday, so I'll plan to do a couple of those before, during and after both of the doubles."

Great!

"And I'll play every note. And this is something I'm planning ahead of time. I'm going to go in and produce these beautiful sounds and everybody's going to go, 'Wow'."

There you go.

"Yeah. That's positive. And I'm just going to make sure that I'm playing my absolute best and we'll just see what happens in Houston."

Why don't we talk toward the end of the week?

"OK. I've got a concert on Friday but I could call you before, at 6:30 my time."

That would be great.

"OK. So I'm playing for a friend on Wednesday. I've got a double on Thursday and I've got a rehearsal and a performance on Friday, and two performances on Saturday. I've got a lot of opportunities. But I don't want to overdo it, either."

Just keep taking forward steps, not worrying about plateauing or peaking early. Don't let that be a concern; we'll take care of it.

"The only reason I bring it up is not to try and be negative about it, but I know that I was putting in three hour plus days before the Detroit audition. I was doing the list maybe twice, maybe three times a day, pulling numbers out of a hat, and I thought I was really moving toward something. And it seems that I kind of burned myself out and I'm aware of that now, but I'm wondering where the fine line is, because I certainly went over it for Detroit."

Just keep moving forward. We have other things we're going to do.

"I didn't exactly take Sunday off, but I did more 'fun' practice and noodled in front of the TV, because I needed it. I really didn't want another hard day. And today I'm motivated. I've gotten good work in. I'm looking forward to getting to the Beethoven."

And I'll look forward to talking to you on Friday.

"OK, Don. Thanks. I'll talk to you then. Bye bye."

CHAPTER SEVEN

VERONICA, TWO DAYS AFTER OUR LAST CONVERSATION. Hi. How're you doing?

"OK...but I'm getting a little bit hyper."

Good.

"Yeah, definitely. I tried my resting pulse. Each day that goes by it increases."

That means you're getting ready for the audition.

"Yup."

So bring me up to date on what you've been doing.

"OK....let's see. I went over to my friend's house yesterday to sing some stuff and it went pretty well. I did three of them, and actually went through the one that's been the hardest for me."

Is that the Bernstein?

"Yes. And it went pretty well."

You sound surprised.

"I know....well, that one went the worst, of course. But even at that, it's just that I'm not focused enough. It's not that it's actually not good, it's just that I don't know how to calm down during that piece yet. But the other pieces went very well and I was not really that nervous. All sorts of things started occurring to me that could go wrong, like 'Oh no, what if I can't do this?', or 'What if I can't do that?' But it all went OK."

What else?

"Let's see....I did my running around and got my pulse up to 120."

Wow!

"Is that a lot?"

That's a lot.

"I did jumping jacks. Then I did the breathing and got it down to an 86."

Veronica, that's fantastic!

"Is it? Oh good!"

That's magnificent!

"Ooooooooo...great!"

How many breaths did it take you?

"It took me...not that many. Let's see.....one, two, three, four, five.....ten... I guess that's not so good."

That's fine.

"Because I did want to make sure that I was relaxed, so I did try to do as many as I needed."

That's the whole idea. It would be nice to take fewer breaths, but the goal is to get your heart rate down. If it takes a few more breaths to do that, it doesn't make that much difference right now. What's critical is getting your heart rate down, and it sounds like you're doing that.

"Right. Ahhhh......and then I sang through a couple of pieces and it was OK. It really is funny to do that in my apartment because I'm not used to having to be on edge like that in my own house. So it was, in a way, like being in an audition, because I wasn't as calm. But it went OK!"

(laughs) What else?

"Ohhhhhhhhh! Let's see.... what else? Umm......Oh, the one thing that's been on my mind is that now I'm getting more nervous about the them announcing the winners at the reception. I sing at eleven in the morning and the reception is at 5:30. Everybody has to be there and they announce who they've accepted. So, having to deal with standing there and possibly not being accepted is really causing me a lot of stress."

Tell me more.

"Uhhhhh....you know, I think it's because I don't really believe that I actually will be accepted. I can see it too easily that I wouldn't be."

How do you see yourself?

"I'm thinking, 'Well, of course you're not going to be accepted. These good things just don't happen to you'. Isn't that awful?"

It's not awful, it's just not helpful.

"But it's just so funny that now I'm getting this stuff. I don't know why."

As the audition gets closer, it may get even more emphatic and louder. It's just part of your normal fears and doubts.

"Normal fears and doubts?"

So remember to keep your sense of humor.

"OK, good. Ooooo...did I tell you that I bought a new dress?"

For the audition or the reception?

"For the audition. So, if nothing else, I can wear my new dress and it's on the stage of the opera house, which is a great opportunity."

That's wonderful. So have you sung the Bernstein yet?

"Yes, I sang it yesterday."

And do you have your cue words?

"Argh! Well, I think I sing it best when I think about 'vowels'. Is that a cue word?"

That could be. What do you mean by "vowels"?

"Well, since it's in English, I think about the words too much and the consonants get in the way of the air going through, and that causes tension in my jaw. So if I just think about 'vowels'... I don't even know if that's going to work necessarily... but the idea is just to let the air through and let it flow."

I really like that! If that's what "vowels" means to you, that's a great cue.

"Maybe I'll just write down what I just said. 'Flow'."

Yeah, just letting it flow. Letting the air go through. That sounds great!

"Yeah, that is better than 'vowels'."

Or just say 'vowels' and 'flow'.

"'Vowels' and 'flow'. That's good. OK."

Now when you're practicing at home, after you get your heart rate up, start practicing with different pieces.

"OK."

How many did you say you were going to sing in Chicago?

"Well, I'll offer four, but most likely they'll pick two and I can pick the first one, so I can control it somewhat."

Have you picked that yet?

"Yeah, the lighter Rossini."

When do they tell you about the second piece?

"After I sing my first one, they deliberate and then they ask for the second one."

I'm going to ask you to make separate index cards for each of the other three pieces. On the cards, write the name of the piece and your cue words. Put them face down on the table by your tape recorder. Turn the recorder on, get your heart rate up, come back into the room, center and get your heart rate down. Use the cue words for the lighter Rossini and then sing it. Then shuffle the other three cards, pick one, read the cue words and say them to yourself, and then sing the piece and nail it.

"Ahhh....that's great. OK! That'll do it."

As soon as you turn the card over, use the words to focus on what you need to do to sing it well. If you want to take a few breaths and center again, that's the time to do it.

"OK, so I can take the amount of time I need?"

Yes.

"That's where I have the time pressure."

Then take two or three breaths. On the first one, focus on your neck and jaw. On the second one, be at your center. And on the third, think about your cue words and project that focused energy to a specific point. You'll have time to do that.

"Yeah, they'll wait."

Veronica, it's all of seven seconds.

(both laugh)

"OK, good. Because then I have a plan for that time, instead of just floundering around and getting nervous."

You've got it! So how's your courage doing?

"Ummmm.....good! The voices, the 'what if's', tried to do some damage yesterday, but they didn't. I still did what I needed to do. When I was singing, they were sure trying. But even with some vocal things that didn't work, I still did them anyway with a lot of courage."

That's wonderful!

"Yeah, I said, 'No! I'm going to do it'. So even things that weren't perfect were OK, and I still went for it."

Good for you!

"Just having something positive to focus on is a big thing to hold on to."

You're right. Let's talk about some other positive things for you to focus on.

"OK."

Did you tell me you've already been to Chicago?

"I've been there once, when I was there for the initial audition."

Do you remember what the hall is like?

"Yeah, pretty much."

This is a good time for you to start imagining yourself backstage, a few minutes before you go on.

"That makes me nervous just thinking about it."

You're going to be nervous, that's for sure. But as you're feeling that, mentally run through your centering and your breathing. Then imagine yourself getting relaxed, focused and walking out...

"Oh noooooo......" (laughs)

...courageously.

"....ahhhhh.....OK. And calmly."

And imagine yourself going through the first Rossini piece, singing it very well.

"So I'm not actually singing it, I'm just going through it in my mind?"

Yes, but try to fully experience what you'd be feeling. If that makes you nervous, then you've got a strategy; do your centering. After your first piece, when you're waiting for them to announce the second, take two or three more breaths and then nail that piece. And after you've walked off, feeling very happy, imagine being congratulated at the reception.

"Yeahhhhh! Oh, OK. Alright!"

Olympic athletes carry it through to standing on top of the awards platform and having a gold medal put around their neck. It's the same thing. It can be very powerful, if you practice it.

"I'll try."

And then the next time you rehearse it, choose a different second piece. I'd like you to keep notes each time you do this, hopefully once or twice a day for the next few days.

"OK, got it. Oh, by the way, I have an audition tonight at seven."

Oh really? This is great!

"It's not anything crucial."

You can use your mental rehearsal practice today to get ready for that.

"OK."

I'd like to talk in the morning about how it goes tonight, so you can tell me the good news.

"Yeah, sure. Of course! They'll probably ask for more than one piece, but I'm going to start with the light Rossini so I can get the feel of starting with that. I wouldn't be surprised if they asked for a second piece. So I can practice doing the other breaths."

That's great, Veronica. One last thing. Between now and the time they tell you you've won on Saturday, I want you to keep unwavering and unfaltering confidence in yourself. Start with a mental set right now that's confident, positive and courageous. Keep that focus tonight and then take that with you to Chicago and into the audition.

"OK. Great!"

And that's it. Just sing like you can tonight and show them what you've got.

"OK. I'll call you tomorrow!"

§

BRIAN. ONE WEEK LATER. Hi. How are you doing?

"I'm doing really well. I've got a concert tonight. I played for some friends on Wednesday and Thursday between rehearsals. They ran me through everything, over an hour of having me out there, and I played most of the stuff very, very well. One of them told me that I was forcing things; part of it may have been the room, but when I got on stage it was much better. I think that getting on stage is a big thing."

What do you mean?

"Well, it's bigger and I don't have to force it, because I have the sense that when I'm on stage, I carry just fine, but when I'm in a small room, sometimes things back up and you just try and use more air, and I end up forcing things. So just between Wednesday and Thursday, it was a major improvement."

In terms of what?

"In terms of concentrating...focusing. I played all the licks quite a bit better. I've been going into rehearsals prepared to play for what I call 'the audience and colleagues that may or may not be listening'. And after my first note, I wanted to make sure that everything was just crystal clear, and everything was really good. And I stayed; I played 45 minutes after rehearsals. I've been playing on stage quite a bit and it's been good for me to stay after and play another forty-five minutes. That felt good too."

That's great!

"And playing in that big room helps."

Is the Houston audition going to be in a big room?

"It'll be on stage. If it's not on stage, I imagine it would be downstairs in this rehearsal room, which is not bad. I've played down there before and it's really got nice acoustics. So if it has to be down there, that wouldn't be so bad. Either way, I could visualize playing down there and playing well."

Last time we talked about naming more of the excerpts.

"Yeah, there are still a few that just escape me, but I've concentrated on how to start each of them. I figured out how to start them more precisely, how to give myself the best entrance, like a pole vaulter getting ready. I need something, not necessarily to pump me up or whatever, but just so that I get a good start. So I named about five or seven more. Some of the excerpts I just look at and I know how to start, some I don't. I only have ten out of the thirty-four that haven't been named yet, so I'm two thirds of the way there."

That's wonderful.

"Three of them are the Schoenbergs that I've played extremely well for my friends. My fellow musicians couldn't find anything wrong with them, but I found a few little flaws."

What did they like about them?

"They were clean...clean and easy. Even though they were technical, I made them sound easy."

There are two good process cues; 'clean' and 'easy'.

"Yeah, I could label the three Schoenbergs that, because I feel the same way about all three of those licks. I could label them all 'clean and easy', or 'clean and easy one', 'clean and easy two', something like that."

Or "clean and easy, one two three". Just put the "post-it" note on each excerpt.

"I've been kind of hit and miss as far as actually putting it there before I play an excerpt, whether it's for myself or for somebody else. I've got to do that more."

Here's the drill. Have someone just randomly pick out excerpts, lay them face down, turn on the tape recorder, leave the room, go through your routine and centering, and then go back into the room with your horn and...

"Do I need to have somebody else there?"

No, you can do this on your own. Just pick two or three from each of the categories, shuffle those, and put them on your music stand. When you turn one over and see what excerpt it is, mentally attach the note to it and experience the thoughts and feelings that go with it. As soon as you say or hear the cue, start playing your best. And then do that again with the next piece.

"OK, so pick six or seven at random. I don't even know what they are before I go out of the room?"

Right.

"I turn the tape deck on , go out of the room and then come in and pick up the first one and look at it. I'll just say for example, 'OK, Beethoven Nine' and automatically picture the 'post-it' note up there, 'tranquil and confident', and then start to play it..."

...as tranquilly and confidently as you can for the first thirty or forty-five seconds. Then once it starts flowing, put that piece down, pick up the next one and do it all over again.

"And this is a way of imprinting my process cues onto the excerpts, with the 'post-it' notes? OK, I like that drill. Yeah, and that's something that I could do after tonight's performance."

You can do this any time and it need not take all that long, because you're only going to be playing short segments, the beginnings of each of the pieces you select at random.

"Right. So in a way, I'm practicing how to start these excerpts, how to put myself in the best frame of mind."

I'd recommend that you do this for about ten minutes at a time. Then take a break and move on to something else. Or shuffle them and start again, so that you go through all sorts of different sequences.

"Yeah, I haven't done that in the last four or five days because I've been playing for other people. I know that burn out is bad and I'm not burned out. I just don't want to go overboard with it."

So we need to keep it fresh.

"Yeah, that's the key; keeping it fresh."

This would be a good time to go through your visualizations.

"Uh huh. I have not been going to the movies as far as, 'OK, I've got five minutes before I go into the room to play my audition', but I do try to get myself nervous, thinking, 'Oh boy, this is it. I don't want to blow this'. I get myself psyched and then do the three centering breaths and bring myself down."

Good! For the visualization of bringing your energy down, see yourself going into the room, turning to the first piece, whatever piece comes to mind, noticing the "post-it" note, seeing yourself starting and playing the entire piece well, and then moving on to the next excerpt.

"OK, so when I go to the movies I want to see myself walking in and playing perfect renditions of these excerpts."

See yourself playing your best through them, finishing well and then walking off happy.

"So go to the movies for Houston, pick two or three excerpts, nail them and walk off happy."

And then stop. Then the next time you do it, say later in the day, at night or the next day, do four or five different pieces. So that by the time you're there, you'll have played every piece at least once, nailing it in your mind.

"That's a good way to go to the movies. I should do this every day. How about twice a day?"

That's ideal.

"Twice every day, maybe mid-morning and the other near bedtime. As a matter of fact, I should probably do that now, before I get dressed. I'm running out of time, but it should be a good one tonight. I actually get a speaking line. It should be pretty interesting."

Really?

"It's the Magic Circle Mime. It's really clever. Basically we come on, the conductor has been killed before the concert even started, and we've got this guy who paid to conduct the orchestra. So he gets to conduct the orchestra, but he also gets killed, and we have to find out who killed these two conductors. It's a lot of 'shtick' and it should be very entertaining. The band is really into it."

Is this the whole orchestra tonight?

"Yup. It's the last Pops series of the season."

And what do you have on Saturday?

"A family concert as well in the morning, so even though it's going to be a beautiful day, I'm not going to get a bike ride tomorrow. I want to make sure that I get some good practicing in, since it's a double concert day. And a good way to not be too tired chopwise is to do this mental practice."

That's a nice shift.

"I've got my list out in front of me now and I still see these blank spaces that I've got to fill in with the process cues. Some of them I don't seem to need, but it couldn't hurt to have one for each of them."

So it's there if you need it.

"I imagine that any process cue is better than none at all. I was a little concerned about not having the proper one, that it might..."

You're right. Having the proper one is not as important as just having one. You can change it anytime. You might come up with a better one in your visualization.

"That's true."

The idea is to have fun and be creative. You can learn within there how to play better.

"Maybe I should make the session for the ones that I haven't named yet and see if something comes to mind."

Start with one of the named ones you like, and then add one or two of the other ones.

"OK, so to get the ball rolling, do ones that I like the phrase of, the 'post-it' note? Right?"

Yes.

"So I have these two mental drills. Well, I have one that's not as much mental, picking the excerpts and turning the tape deck on, doing my whole pre-audition routine, then going in and applying the notes and then playing the pieces."

Making sure those phrases get you off to a good start, because after that you're pretty much are on cruise control.

"Yeah, once I get things going, there's no stopping me."

So you're just going to rehearse getting the ball rolling, knowing that your skill and talent will take over after that.

"Yeah, my best auditions have been when I've started well and then my confidence builds with each excerpt."

That's the feeling to have in Houston with every excerpt; that with each one, you're saying....

"...Yeah! I can do this. I can nail this one."

Alright! You've got it. When can we talk again?

"We could talk maybe Monday or Tuesday. I can tell you how the weekend went."

How about Tuesday evening?

"6:30 my time?"

That's good for me.

"OK. And I will fill you in on what the movies are like."

Keep in mind that we're still making some subtle shifts.

"Right. I'm not going to get stale. A lot of these licks I'm nailing physically, but I'd like to get them more solid mentally as well."

Which is what we're moving toward.

"Yeah, I can see that. That's good. Before I forget, I'm going to write all of this down. I've got to drill and go to the movies in Houston. That ought to give me plenty to do."

Play well tonight, Brian. I look forward to talking with you next week.

"Likewise. Thanks, Don."

You're welcome. Bye bye.

"Bye."

CHAPTER EIGHT

Veronica, the next morning. "OK. So I did the things we talked about, rehearsing the whole thing in my mind."

How'd it go?

"OK..."

OK or good?

"Parts of it were really good, but there are little parts of it that I really have to work on, like when I'm walking out. I had trouble with that one, just imagining myself walking out in a great, confident manner."

Ahhh. Stay with that.

"Argh! You know, I can picture myself walking out like, 'Hi! Hi! I'm here to sing!' and being very excited and hyper about it. But I don't want to do that. I just want to walk out in a strong way, you know, and they just happen to be there."

Wonderful! And the rest of it?

"Ahhhh....good! Very good."

You imagined yourself singing well and walking off feeling happy?

"Yes. Yes. And then I did a little visualization of whatever last night was going to be, and I got the index cards and I made them all kinds of funny designs. Is that good?"

That's really good!

"Each one has its own character that kind of reflects the piece. Then I wrote my words on it. So now I can sort of visualize the card itself."

Perfect!

"So, on the way to the audition, I ran into some friends on the train. They were going too. I showed them my index cards. They thought that was great."

(both laugh)

"Ummm....so I sang and, let's see.....where do I start? There are a couple of things I want to talk about. I sang well...I was tired, but I still thought that I sang pretty well."

Uh huh....

"And I was able to keep my concentration pretty well. The only thing I noticed in the first piece was, whenever I would start to get a little unsure of myself, I'd start looking at the floor. I just don't think that's a good idea."

You mean while you're actually singing?

"Yeah. Whenever I was unsure of myself, either vocally or with what the character was doing, I would just lower my eyes a little bit, and I don't want to do that."

What would you rather do?

"Well, I don't know, I think I should look straight out. Because if you're looking at the floor, the audience can't see you. I don't know if it really takes away from the performance, but I noticed that I did it every time I was feeling a little insecure about something."

How many times was that?

"Four."

During one piece?

"Yeah."

Was that during the Rossini?

"Yes. I think it came more from what the character would be thinking about, rather than vocal problems. I may have to do some work on that. And then the second piece they asked for was the Bernstein."

Good!

(both laugh)

I called them and I told them to do that.

"You did?! (laughs harder) But I was kind of surprised. I thought they would ask for *Carmen,* but you never know. So....I remembered my words, luckily, and took time to take a couple breaths...which was no problem, taking the time."

Great.

"And I can just say, even though I was tired, it was still pretty good. So that was that. I didn't know what they thought of me, but I don't particularly care."

What did you think about your performance?

"I thought I was good!"

When you did the Bernstein piece, did you use 'vowels' and 'flow'?

"Yeah, in a lot of places. There was one place I didn't. But I started out doing that."

Do you feel it got you off to a good start?

"Yes. Definitely. And I remember one part, just before there's a kind of crazy middle section where you have to sing a lot of high notes, I just kept calming myself down because you have to be very calm before you sing that. And it worked."

How'd you do that?

"I think I thought of just taking control of the tempo and calming it down, so that I would be in a place where I would be ready to sing it."

I like that. How are the 'what if's' doing?

"Oh, God! I don't know....I'm really just pushing them aside, but it's hard, because in some ways you can take comfort in hearing them and it's very hard to push them away. But I keep doing it."

Why is there comfort in what they have to say?

"I don't know. After last night's audition, I thought, 'Gee, that was pretty good'. And I thought, 'Why aren't these people just jumping up and down for joy that they were able to hear me sing?'. But they weren't jumping up and down. They were like, 'Oh great, great. Nice. OK, good.' I think they should be jumping up and down for joy, and they just weren't doing that. And so I thought, 'Well, am I crazy?' I must be crazy!"

Well, you're certainly not, but you have no control over anyone else's responses. How do you know they didn't have a fight with their spouse that morning or that their house hadn't gone into foreclosure?

"Oh, yeah. I see what you mean."

Don't take it personally. It probably had nothing to do with you, and trying to control it is a waste of time and energy and distracts you out of your center.

"Right."

I mean, they may not like your hair. Maybe they were looking for a blonde. And that has nothing to do with you.

"I guess not."

Things that are under our control make us feel more comfortable and secure. Trying to control things that are out of our control make us nervous. Do you agree with that?

"Oh yeah, yeah."

So pay attention to the things you can control, like your breathing, self-talk, your cue words and focus. Take care of those things and let go of the things that are out of your control.

"Right!"

Other's responses to you or your singing or what your character is supposed to be doing is somewhat out of your control. I shouldn't say out of your control, but it's not under your control.

"Right. I can't make them like me."

No. That's exactly it. All you can do is do your best.

"Ohhhhh!"

I'm sorry, but this is reality. You need to accept that. All you can do is go in there and do your best.

"That's kind of a relief in a way."

It's just like critics. You really can't control what they say. Can you accept that?

"I think I have to. Because I always think, 'What if I sing my best? Then everybody will know how great I am'. But I've never sung my best, really."

So back to the 'what if's.' I'm still wondering why they're still comforting to you. I guess they'll be going to Chicago with you.

"Oh God! I don't want them to come to Chicago with me."

Well, they're going to go. They've already booked the flight.

(both laugh)

"I don't know where they get the money."

They might be sitting in first class.

"Right!" (more laughter)

How's your unwavering confidence doing?

"Oh, God! Oh, God! (laughs) That was exhausting, very hard. But I did it for most of the day yesterday and then I had it when I got back from the audition."

Please keep that up through Saturday.

"Sunday."

I thought the audition was Saturday.

"Well, it's Saturday and Sunday. Saturday I fly in and meet with them and talk with them and then Sunday morning I sing. So it's both days."

So you don't sing on Saturday?

"I'll have a coaching, but not any kind of audition."

Who coaches you?

"Whoever will be playing the piano for me on Sunday. One of their staff."

Just so you can get in synch?

"Yeah. Talk about whatever things the piece has."

After that, you may want to update your process cues. And then, when you get back to your hotel room, mentally rehearse your centering and performance, using those cues. Oh, you should also change the index cards.

"Oh...(laughs)...but they're so pretty."

Make more pretty ones.

"OK."

Let see, what else. Back to your eyes...is the centering working? Are you pleased with the breathing?

"I am, I am."

Was it nine or ten breaths before you went on?

"Oh no. I did about five."

And five got you there?

"Yeah. Well, maybe it didn't really get me there, but I felt like I was ready to sing."

What do you mean by not really there?

"I don't know…(laughs)…I was breathing, but I didn't have my mind on it like I had before…as much".

But that's the whole idea, to get your mind on it. Don't just go through the motions. It's supposed to capture your attention on one thing in the middle of a storm swirling around you. You should feel like you're at the eye of the storm. It should be relatively calm there, in spite of everything that's going on around you. You can take a break from that if you're not caught up in it. Just get back to being at your center.

"So, at some point, just before I have to walk out…"

Take the time. In fact, give yourself extra time; you don't want to rush it.

"So be able to time it, because I'll know who goes before me. And when they're finishing up…"

That's right. It will work for you if you use it.

"I have a feeling that the minute I walk into the theatre, I'll probably want to be starting that."

Allow yourself the time to do that.

"OK."

Before you did the Bernstein piece, what did you do?

"I took three breaths. Is that enough?"

You tell me. Was it enough?

"I took one breath for each word and then one breath just to feel that I was at my center."

Were you?

"Yeah, I think I was."

And that set you up to start the piece well?

"Yeah. And I felt pretty grounded for that. But beforehand, it was kind of crazy. I have a habit of talking to people too much..."

...and spinning out?

"Yup."

Let's go back to your third sequence of breaths. After you've gotten in touch with your center, you were going to breathe and say your cues words and then open your eyes and project that energy out to a point. Did you find a point?

"You know...I didn't. (laughs) So to a specific place?"

Imagine standing where you're going to be singing, so you can figure out the best place to direct that energy.

"Alright, got it."

Now imagine tacking your index cards up right there.

"I think you lost me."

Before you go in to sing, when nothing's going on, find the place where you'll be standing.

"You mean...actually, physically go out on stage?"

Yes. And as you're standing there, look out and find a place on the wall or a curtain out in the theater, wherever your voice would best go. Once you find that, imagine tacking up your index cards and then projecting your voice out there.

"Oh, out to that place."

And then, when you do go on stage to sing, there are your cards. And rather than looking at the floor...

"...look at the cards. Great! I'll have a place to go."

A place that will remind you of what you want to do. And with your new, fancy cards, it's a friendly place. The floor can't offer that.

"I don't know why I look at the floor. I don't do that when I'm performing. I only do that in auditions."

So when you're doing your mental rehearsals for the audition, imagine directing your focus out there. It will look a lot better to those watching.

"Great. I'm all excited now."

So you're all set.

"I am?"

Yeah. But...you're not perfect.

"No."

And you're probably not going to sing perfectly. I just want you to do what you're been doing. That's all you need to do, Veronica. Just remember that you've prepared and when you do step on stage, you'll be ready. All you have to do then is do what you've been practicing and rehearsing and you'll be fine.

"OK. I believe it."

Good. Good. You've made some incredibly wonderful strides.

"Yeah. This has been great."

And you're going to be nervous, but you've got ways to deal with it. You've got a great strategy designed to get you centered, not worrying about outside things or other people. Continually go there, do your breathing and remember your cue words. Don't just go through the motions. Really hold on to them, get their value and then project that energy out to your cards.

"OK."

So basically we've got a big feedback loop between you, your center and your cards, which brings you back to your cue words inside you.

"Aha!"

And it's just you and you and you.

"Oh, that's great. OK."

Within that big loop or circle, you can do just fine; and you will.

"OK. Yeah, that's very easy to picture. Oh, I can't wait to go try it. I want to do it now and get it over with!"

(both laugh)

So if you have some time today, continue to go through some situations and shuffle the cards and then practice putting the card out there and, if you get into any difficult spots in any of the pieces, simply find your cards. In fact, for today, if you're going to do it at home, I would literally find a far wall and...

"Stick them up there?"

Yeah!

"Yeah, that's what I'll do."

OK! I'm proud of you. You're doing great!

"Oh, thank you. I'm so excited. I can't wait to try it."

So say 'hi' to the 'what if's' on the plane. Go up to first class and visit them.

"Oh, I will. I'm going to give them a copy of my cards to enjoy." (both laugh)

"So I'll probably speak with you tomorrow night."

Hopefully so. Have a safe trip to Chicago.

"I will."

I'll talk to you tomorrow, Veronica. Bye bye.

"Good bye."

❧

BRIAN. A WEEK LATER. How's it going?

"Really good. Yesterday was my last big day at work. I played a good audition for another friend; he put me through my paces very quickly. He's one of the better players in the band, so he made me a little nervous. Other times I would have lost a little focus, but not this time. He pointed out some different technical things, so each time I do this, I get a little something extra."

Great!

"But I figured that would be the last time I do that before Houston. I don't need to work on too many things at once. I find that I end up working on nothing or try to do too many things. The brain can only do one thing at a time, basically. So I have all my process cues written out and they are just how I'm going to start it. I know how the piece starts and then I have rhythmic subdivisions, and for some of them I have what happens just beforehand. I think of that and I think in the rhythm. Like for the Beethoven *Eroica* Trio, the first phrase starts after a gear shift of tempo, and that sometimes throws me off. So I decided I'm just going to take it where I know the tempo ought to be and then transfer that to the beginning. That works pretty well for me."

Good!

"I spent about four hours practicing yesterday, including the session with my friend. So now I think I need to taper off."

Let me explain something in athletic terms. Let's take springboard divers who've been practicing their eleven competition dives over and over again. Early and mid-way through the season, they will do each dive three or four times, then move on to the next dive in sequence and do that one three or four times. As they get closer to the competition though, they start doing what's called "lists". They do only one of each dive and then move on to the next dive, the same as they'll be doing in the competition. When they're cutting back or "tapering" this way, it frees up some time. They can use that extra time to do mental preparation and mental rehearsal, and back off on the physical repetitions. So I would say the same for you. Have short run-throughs of the excerpts. Turn on the tape recorder, go through your preparation and centering, come in and play forty-five seconds of first the random pick, and then pick the next excerpt. Try to do ten or fifteen pieces like this.

"So turn the tape deck on, go out, come back in and play a random list. Just 'one time only practicing' as I like to call it."

Yes, and after ten or fifteen minutes, stop and go on to something else and come back to it later.

"So I should still do a few of those before Houston. See, I don't want the effort to get stale."

No, you don't want them to get stale at all.

"Am I still practicing the process cues?"

You're still using the 'post-it' phrases with the beginning of the pieces. You're rehearsing that process?

"Yeah, that takes the emphasis off, 'Oh no, here's this one!' A lot of them are very positive. Most of the ones I played for my friend were like, 'Alright, let's do this!' and, 'Yeah, I'm ready to go with this one'. That's a good sign to me."

That's a great sign.

"But he did find a few things at fault and had some comments."

That's fine.

"Yeah, that was good. He wasn't sure how much to nail me, but I was thinking that this is what I need, because they're going to do the same thing in Houston. OK, so I can do this. I guess I have a little bit of today. We have a concert tonight and I would have tomorrow. Yeah, basically all I have is tomorrow. What should I do about Sunday? My flight gets in there about two in the afternoon. I'll be playing around 10:30, Monday morning."

I wouldn't do a whole lot of practicing on Sunday.

"I was planning on taking most of the day off."

Good!

"Just do a little bit of playing."

And get yourself acclimated, obviously drink a lot of water, walk around, shake it out, stay loose.

"Yeah, I'm going to drink on the plane...I mean water!"

And if you do have any nervous thoughts, just remember all the work that you've done. And it's all done.

"Yeah, I had some of those today. After the rehearsal, I started having my first pre-audition anxious feelings."

Ah. Normal fears and doubts.

"Yeah, I've got them."

Well then, just say, 'Hi. I'm glad to see you again, but this time I'm prepared.'

"My old friend. I guess I still have some work to do. I wish I had a little more time, but I think I always think that when I come to an audition."

Even if you had another six months, Brian, at the end of that time you'd still probably want another couple weeks.

"Probably!"

I know with race car drivers, they're always going over the track one more time and refining the points where they're going to shift and brake and where they can pass. I was eating supper with one of the drivers the night before the Miami Grand Prix, and he said, "What should I do tonight? Should I go over the track one more time?". I told him that he was as prepared as he was going to get, and that the best thing for him to do was to relax, knowing that when the flag went down in the morning, he'd be ready. I'll say the same thing to you. You're ready.

"Yeah, I mean, I'm pretty ready. My chops are in great shape and my brain has never been in better shape, thanks to you. So Sunday night, just know that I'm ready and kick back?"

And if you have a "what if", think, 'No, I've done my preparation' and see yourself going through the centering, using the process cues and then nailing it.

"And then Monday just get up, warm up and walk in and do it."

Do what you've been rehearsing.

"Do you want me to call you on Sunday?"

I'm not sure if I'm going to be home. But I'm just going to tell you to have fun and remind you to do what you've been doing. The goal is not to try to play perfectly, but to play optimally. The best you can, given the extreme circumstances. This is not the time to try for a peak experience. The goal is not to play over your head or try to even to reproduce the absolute best you've ever done in your whole life. Just play the way you've been playing recently.

"I need to give myself permission to play like Brian."

Please don't try to do anything else, because you haven't practiced that.

"Yeah, play like me. My goal is to go out there and lay it down for them and play like I know I can. And they'll like it."

And that's all you can do, Brian. No extra pressure.

"I hope not! I think if I do that, they will like it. So just know that I'm ready and kick back and get used to the place, relax and maybe do a little more visualization."

And if you do feel any anxiety, just do a quick visualization of seeing yourself nailing this piece or playing that excerpt well.

"So, be prepared for my old friend. Do you think that might

happen?"

Do I think he'll be there? He wouldn't miss it! But you know what to do.

"Yeah. Just counter the negative with, 'This time, it's going to be like this', and remind myself that this is how I can play if I just allow myself. Alright. So I have a little bit of time tonight and then I've got most of the day tomorrow and then I leave."

Can you try to call me after you get into Houston?

"Yeah, the flight gets in around two."

Sounds like you're ready, Brian. You just need to do what you've been doing.

"Yeah...I'm pretty ready....maybe some more visualization. I've been seeing myself walking into the musician's entrance door, signing in and just chilling out and focusing...and when they knock on the door, I just get my horn and walk in. I know the feeling very well. So I walk in...they usually give you the instructions. They say, 'Don't talk to the committee, blah blah blah'. I've done this enough times. And then I imagine walking out into the big hall and sitting down and getting myself centered and ready...looking at the excerpt and having this feeling of, 'I know how to do this' and then nailing it. How's that sound?"

Great! And if, in the middle, you feel anything, just take one or two centering breaths and get your focus back and then continue.

"With the last run through with my friend, even though I wasn't particularly nervous, a couple of notes shook. I was trying to stay relaxed, but I was probably not as relaxed as I should have been. That's a sure sign that I've got too much tension, especially on some of the low notes."

So maybe take a little time after you get there and put some pressure on yourself to play some difficult low notes and then get centered before you go for it.

"So that still works. You see, I was going to taper off on practicing."

I'm just asking you to do some fine tuning with those notes.

"OK, just a little bit. Alright, so I'll do a little fine tune practice with my steady low notes. I figure with the concerts tonight and tomorrow, my chops will be ready for a break on Sunday. But a little fine tuning certainly isn't going to hurt, especially down low, it's not going to blow them out. OK, so I will give you a call probably Sunday evening. I will work on this stuff."

I look forward to talking with you then. Brian, I want you to know that you're ready. You're at an optimal level.

"Yeah, I'm about as ready as I'm going to be."

So have some fun tonight.

"Yeah I will. You know, everything I've learned preparing for this audition I can put into use for my regular playing as well. Thanks again, Don."

You're very welcome. Have a good flight.

"OK. I'll stay hydrated. And I'll talk to you when I get there."

CHAPTER NINE

VERONICA, THE NEXT DAY. Hi! How's Chicago?

"Ohhhh, it's OK......ohhhhhh.......pretty scary!"

Do you get some sleep last night?

"Nope. I tried. I tried."

I'm sorry.

"I think I will tonight."

Good.

"Yeah, it was a long day. I was very scattered. I met with the pianist and did the coaching. I didn't prepare very well for the coaching, I mean, in my mind. And so I didn't do what I wanted to do with my pieces, but I figure that's OK, because I will tomorrow."

There you go!

"It was just a long day and I'm tired. I figure I'd just go through the whole process. I know exactly how the process is going to go. I don't know exactly what pieces they're going to pick, but I figured I'd go through it in my mind before I go to bed and then get ready in the morning and go do it."

What time do you sing?

"11:15."

So are you nervous enough?

"Ummmm....I don't think I'm that nervous right now. Now that I'm here and it's inevitably going to happen, I certainly want to sing well. I really want to get enough rest so that my voice feels fresh. I want to be in control and do what I want to do."

Oh good!

"I really do! I think I get a little nervous, even though I don't feel it. I don't want to say hysterical; it's not quite that much. It's just a little scattered, I guess, so it's difficult to just focus on what I have to do because a million other thoughts come into my mind."

Then get back to the hub....

"Uh huh...."

....and focus on what you need to do, which is get centered and sing well.

"Yeah, in my new dress."

(both laugh)

That's it, in your new dress.

"That's what I need. I didn't have my dress on today!"

(both laugh)

"Ohhhhhhhhh gosh! And it's really unnerving to just fly in early in the morning and then have to be all fresh in the afternoon and be in a strange hotel. It's tough to stay positive."

But there's your job. You've got to fight for it.

"Exactly."

And the unalterable, unwavering confidence?

"That's it!"

Please use everything you've rehearsed.

"Uh huh."

And put the index cards up in your mind and use all the stuff we've discussed. It will work very well for you.

"Yeah. I think that the index cards are going to be pretty crucial because one of the heads of the program said, 'Well, you're going to walk out on that stage and you're going to look out into the audience and that theater is so huge, it's going to look like the jaws of hell'. Argh!"

(both laugh)

You'll just see your index cards. Everybody else can see the jaws of hell.

(both laugh)

"I'll make my index cards really big."

Good.

"I really think today was the hardest day, just coming in and seeing people. And then tomorrow, I just need to do my thing. That's really what I'm ready to do."

So I think you're a little bit nervous, and that's fine, because you're ready.

"Well, I'm excited to do it. I really am."

Just make sure you wear your new dress.

"OK!"

(both laugh)

Well, that's it.

"Ready to go."

If I can, I'll try to call you. I want to hear the good news.

"Yeaaaa! Don, thanks for checking in with me."

I'll talk to you tomorrow, Veronica.

"OK. Bye."

Bye bye.

ⓢ

BRIAN. PHONE MESSAGE, THE FOLLOWING SUNDAY. "Hi, Don. I'm in Houston at the Double Tree. It's 11:15 here, way late for you to call me back. But I just wanted to let you know that everything's going great. I feel good; I'm prepared; I've got a good mental focus. So I'm just going to go in and do everything we talked about and I will let you know how it all goes. So thanks for all your help and I'll be talking with you really soon."

CHAPTER TEN

VERONICA, THE NEXT EVENING. "Hello."

Hi, Veronica. It's Don. How are you?

"Good! How are you?"

Fine. Tell me about your day.

"It was great! It was great! I got the job!"

Congratulations!

"I got it. I'm in shock! (laughs) I keep on looking at the contract and making sure it's my name, because I can't believe it."

Oh...you turkey.

"I know. (laughs) So it was a good day. I got some good sleep last night and I got up and took my time and then got ready and put on my dress. Oh, I had the greatest dream though. I had a dream that I got to the audition and I took off my coat...and I...I...I didn't...I had a different dress on...I had the wrong dress on." (laughs)

An anxiety dream.

"Yeah. It was really good. Then someone had to give me another dress and it wasn't quite right, and I didn't have time to warm up and it was just, you know...when I woke up I was very relieved that I still had a chance to go to the audition. (laughs) So I went in and sang and I did what I wanted to do."

Which pieces did you sing?

"I sang the lighter Rossini first and then I walked off. They heard everybody and then they had me come back to sing a second piece. They asked for the Bernstein. It was good though, because I really started being chatty with people before, and then I walked off to the side and went through my centering, like three times..."

Good, good.

"...and then I went out and did it. But I tell you, this afternoon at the reception, just waiting to find out, was ten times more stressful than the singing. They had us all in this room and they made us wait an hour before they announced who they would be taking into the program. But I was standing there and they announced my name."

Congratulations! That's wonderful.

"Thanks. I really was able to do what I wanted. I really did what I wanted and I took those breaths. I just took the breaths and I thought of the cue words and I looked up...and the theatre was not the jaws of hell....it was really very nice, actually... and it really made all the difference, because I was in control. And I took as much time as I wanted. It became a really powerful thing to just say, 'I am out here now, this is my time.' It felt great."

Veronica, that's a huge step forward.

"So it really helped me and I was able, in a very stressful situation, to be nice to myself about it."

Hey! Another big step!

"Oh...unheard of. "

Did you put the index cards up?

"Yes, I did. What happened was....I made a big card...last night before I went to bed. I was getting really scared and I made an index card that just said 'Courage!' on it....with exclamation points... because sometimes...the cards were....everytime I started looking at the cards, they started making me nervous...the cards started making me nervous. So I just made this one..."

'Courage!'

"...and I think that was the card I was looking at, because I said...'You can't lose... if you're being courageous.' And anytime I would feel myself getting nervous, I just fought for it. I fought for having enough breath and fought for really...really doing it. Ohhhhhhhhhhh."

I'm proud of you.

"Oh, God!"

You did it.

"I did it. And I can't believe it. I can't believe it. (laughs) Maybe it was the dress though, and not me."

I want a picture of you in that dress.

"Me in my winning dress? OK, I would be thrilled."

Thanks.

"No, thank you. It really made all the difference in the world for me to be in control of an audition for once. I know I've still got a lot to work on, of course...but this is a big job. This is the biggest thing I've ever gotten and it was so important. I can't believe it. So this is work for a year."

This is a year contract?

"Yeah. I have to move back here in March. It's a little scary, but it's OK."

Hey, you've got courage.

"Exactly...I've got that index card."

You can take that to Chicago with you.

"I think so. Hey, it's starting to hit me...I've got a job for the next year! Wow! This really made all the difference. It really moved me up to a different level of singing. Because the other singers there were really very good...and you just had to have something else."

Well, you do. Maybe we can talk in a few days, after you come down. Congratulations. I'm so proud of you.

"Thank you, thank you."

Well, you take care, Veronica.

"I'll call you next week."

OK. Bye bye.

☙

BRIAN. PHONE MESSAGE TWO DAYS LATER. "Hey, Don. I tried to leave word with you yesterday, but your answering machine said you were out of town, so I guess I'll just have to leave this on your machine. I think you'll be happy to know that I am the new second horn of the Houston Symphony."

(Cheers and clapping in the background)

"I'm very pleased about that and I think you will be also. I would love to talk to you. I'll be here until Sunday, so please give me a call when you can and I'll give you all the details. It still hasn't sunk in yet. Hope to talk to you soon. Thanks. Bye bye."

CHAPTER ELEVEN

VERONICA, A WEEK AFTER SHE GOT BACK FROM CHICAGO.
"Hello, Don."

Hi. How are you?

"Ahhhhh....OK. I'm so used to having this high energy problem and trying to calm myself down. I'm having the opposite problem now. I have this audition tomorrow and I'm like, 'What am I doing. I'm too tired. I can't get up for it. And they won't want to give you a job anyway. And you're just the same as last year. You can work as hard as you want, but you're still not good'. Oh, I know who those voices are, but I told them to go away." (laughs)

And they didn't go away?

"No, they didn't go away! Oh, God! And I had to learn this brand new piece. The audition was supposed to be yesterday and I found out the night before that it was the next day, and I had to learn a new piece. It's basically singing a nursery rhyme. It's really not much harder than that. But it still requires the same amount of concentration and commitment if you're going to get up and sing anything, even if it's a scale, in front of people."

OK.

"I know this is a lot of little things. So I learned the new piece and I went through it and made an index card for it. This is my best index card yet! I love it. It's the sweetest looking thing because it's a very funny little song. And it's so cute, it makes me happy."

Great!

"But sometimes I look at the card and I walk away and think, 'Well, the card's good but I'm not'. I just think that I should walk into the audition and give them the card."

(both laugh)

Good idea.

"Yeah, really. I'm so lethargic about this next audition. I'm just down about it."

What's it for?

"It's for the Orchestra of St. Luke's. They do a children's opera every year in October and November. It's pretty good money and the timing's really good. It's a good orchestra and it seems like I would be perfect for it. A friend called and said they were having call-backs this week. They weren't happy with the mezzos they had heard and asked her about me. So I already know, going in, that they don't even really like the people that have call-backs, and if I look at it objectively, I would be great, but I can't. Some part of me has to say, 'No. It's wrong for me to believe that I would be right for it'. I don't know."

Do you want it?

"Yeah, I would. But I just can't seem to get up for it."

Well, you ran your activation engine at a high rev rate for a long time.

"Yeah!"

You burned a lot of fuel and now you're feeling low energy. You and I have worked on controlling the energy that's been too high. You did a good job with that. Now it's time to come at it from a point of low energy. You're not always going to have high energy, but that shouldn't stop you from singing well. Sometimes your engine's going to be slowed down.

"But I want it to be a positive place, like I was in Chicago. That was a really great place; I was excited and couldn't wait to sing."

But you can still sing well, even though you're not feeling tons of energy. You've got to realize that your good singing is somewhat independent of your energy levels. You can do it with a lot of adrenalin; you can do it when you're not up that much; you can do it when you're tired. The essential thing is that you can do it from wherever you are, as long as you're centered.

"Right. I know I can. I just have to trust that a little more."

Yes, but it's just a little bit harder to do when you're feeling low energy.

"You know, I'll be OK. I'll get through the night."

And in the meantime, let your energy be low. You don't need it up until you get there. And when you do, you're going to experience normal fears and doubts. Your activation level will go up and that will bring you up to a different place. The essential thing is to focus on singing your best, which comes from being centered and singing from inside-out.

"Yeah, OK. Well I did it this morning after breakfast. I was like, 'I'm just too tired to sing. I can't practice', but I did just that. I did some breathing and centering, and then started practicing and it worked, even though I was not really feeling that great. You just have to be a little more concentrated about it. And it came out fine. I got some good work done. But it was exhausting."

I figured that inevitably, some of that high energy would burn off and you would drop below the curve.

"Oh, God! It's been terrible, terrible. I wish I could keep that energy up all the time."

You can't. You just can't.

"No, I can't. And then I give myself a hard time because I can't understand what's wrong."

So get some rest today, let the adrenalin kick in tonight, sing your best and then get some more rest.

"Alright."

Maybe we can talk over the weekend or sometime next week.

"Oh, good."

Please keep the same routine before you go in. Go through the process.

"OK. Thanks, Don. I'll let call you and let you know how it went."

That sounds good, Veronica. I'll talk to you then.

"Take care. Bye bye."

§

BRIAN. PHONE MESSAGE, THREE MONTHS LATER. "Hello Don, this is Brian. I'm in Houston. It's Saturday afternoon and I wanted to talk to you about the next couple of weeks before my first rehearsals and performances. I'm only going to be here for a few hours, then I'm going to see a movie with some buddies. I'm pretty well settled and I had a good practice session today. It's been a little rough; I have to get my air going and get my chops going again. I have a gig next week, so I'm getting motivated now. I'm ready to start working with you again. I hope everything's going well and I'll speak with you soon. Bye bye."

CHAPTER TWELVE

VERONICA, THE NEXT DAY. "Hi, Don. How are you?"

Fine. How did it go?

"I just got the phone call."

Well...?

"Well...there was a message on my machine and I just called them back and they gave me the details. So, exactly what you said would happen, happened. The nervous energy just kicked in and I actually had to calm myself down. They were very nice and I was in control and it was fun. And I left there feeling like if I don't get the job, it has nothing to do with me, because I was really great. But I got it!"

That's wonderful. Congratulations!

"Oh, thank you. And thanks for talking to me yesterday. That really helped."

You're welcome. Please remember to send me the picture of you in that black dress.

"OK, I will. I'll talk with you soon."

Great! Bye bye.

EPILOGUE

S EVERAL WEEKS EARLIER, Brian had stopped in Lake George to visit. We went to a local park where we spent the afternoon working on peak performance skills and trying different ways to effect flow states. It was much different than the skills we had worked on in preparing for the Houston audition. We learned that afternoon that an essential skill for Brian would be letting go. I asked him to play more freely, without concern for missing notes. I even suggested he play some "clams" on purpose. He didn't like the exercise.

We tried a number of things that afternoon in the park, like painting pictures with his sound and playing around casually with different kinds of music, like Irish folk tunes. I'm not exactly sure what eventually turned the key, but he really got "there" and we both heard it immediately. It was incredible! Getting there more often would become a priority after he got settled in Houston. In the meantime, he would be driving back to Syracuse, packing up and moving. I would be spending the next week with the Lake George Opera.

I've stayed in touch with Ed in the years since we met on the golf course in Colorado. He's still the principal bass with the Syracuse Symphony. His handicap has come down four strokes since then. Last summer, he won his club championship for the second year in a row.

Veronica is back in New York and doing really well. I heard her sing not long ago and she sounded great! Brian and I have stayed in touch over the years. He's still with the Houston Symphony and we've continued our work together, as we both learn and grow.

I'm getting ready to go back to Lake George for my third season. I moved to Manhattan last September, so I could work more effectively with my artists in person (no longer on the phone). Since then, I've been very fortunate. The artists with whom I have worked continue to win major competitions and important jobs, including Artist of the Year honors with the Syracuse Opera and the principal horn position with the Syracuse Symphony.

That brings it full circle.

ABOUT THE AUTHOR

DON GREENE was a nationally ranked high school diver from Long Island, who competed for the West Point swimming team. After graduation and Ranger training, he served in the Army's Green Berets. He has a Master's Degree and Doctorate in Sports Psychology. His doctoral dissertation demonstrated how police SWAT officers could improve their shooting performance under high stress by using techniques that worked well with competitive athletes.

Dr. Don Greene was the Sports Psychologist for the U.S. Olympic Diving Team, which included medalists Greg Louganis and Michele Mitchell. He also served on the staff of the World Championship Swimming Team, Golf Digest, and the Vail Ski School. He worked for more than a decade with professional golfers, tennis players and Grand Prix racecar drivers before beginning to work with performing artists.

In the past five years, Dr. Greene's clients have won numerous auditions and competitions. In the 1997 Met audition for horn, of the 59 competitors, his artists placed first, second, fourth and fifth! Now based in Manhattan, he counsels individual artists and teaches at the Juilliard School. He is on the staff of the Lake George Opera Festival and OperaWorks Intensive Programs, and conducts master classes for the New World Symphony.

For more information on Dr. Greene's workshops or
to order the Artist's Profiles, please write or fax:

330 West 56th Street, #7-L
New York, NY 10019
Fax (212) 246-9739

DEMCO